## On the cover:

The **northern spotted owl** is one of the largest owls in North America. Its population has been decreasing drastically as a result of a declining forest habitat. Only about 560 pairs of owls still live in northern California. Northern spotted owls have a unique flight pattern which involves a series of quick wingbeats followed by a gliding flight. This pattern allows the owls to glide silently down upon their prey.

# California Treasures

## A Reading/Language Arts Program

### Program Authors

Diane August
Donald R. Bear
Janice A. Dole
Jana Echevarria
Douglas Fisher
David Francis
Vicki Gibson
Jan E. Hasbrouck
Scott G. Paris
Timothy Shanahan
Josefina V. Tinajero

 **Macmillan/McGraw-Hill**

## Contributors

Time Magazine, The Writers' Express, Accelerated Reader

Students with print disabilities may be eligible to obtain an accessible, audio version of the pupil edition of this textbook. Please call Recording for the Blind & Dyslexic at 1-800-221-4792 for complete information.

B

The McGraw·Hill Companies

### Macmillan/McGraw-Hill

Published by Macmillan/McGraw-Hill, of McGraw-Hill Education, a division of The McGraw-Hill Companies, Inc., Two Penn Plaza, New York, New York 10121.

Printed in the United States of America

ISBN: 978-0-02-199969-9/3, Bk. 2
MHID: 0-02-199969-4/3, Bk. 2
2 3 4 5 6 7 8 9 (079/055) 12 11 10 09

# Welcome to
# California *Treasures*

**I**magine raising butterflies at the edge of a rain forest, learning about penguin chicks in Antarctica, or reading about a rooster that likes to cook. Your **Student Book** contains these and other award-winning fiction and nonfiction selections.

## *Treasures* Meets California Standards

The instruction provided with each reading selection in your **Student Book** will ensure that you meet all the **California Reading/Language Arts Standards** for your grade. Throughout the book, special symbols (such as ✔) and codes (such as **R 1.1.2**) have been added to show where and how these standards are being met. They will help you know *what* you are learning and *why*.

## What do these symbols mean?

**CA** = Tested Standards in California

✔ = Skill or Strategy that will appear on your test

**R** = Reading Standards

**W** = Writing Standards

**LC** = Language Conventions Standards

**LAS** = Listening and Speaking Standards

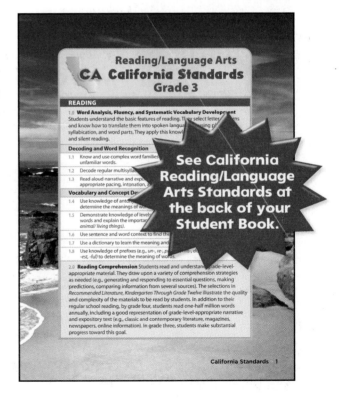

 **Macmillan/McGraw-Hill**

# Unit 5

## Science
# Those Amazing Animals

Award Winning Selection

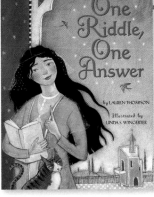

# Unit 4
## Our Teams

## The Big Question

### What makes a strong team?

Theme Launcher Video

 LOG ON ▶  Find out more about what makes a strong team at **www.macmillanmh.com**.

A team is a group of people who work together to get a job done. There are many different kinds of teams, such as sports teams. But did you know that a family is a team? Members of a band are a team. Students in a classroom are a team, too. There are teams of doctors, engineers, and scientists.

A team is strong when its members work together and help each other out. A strong basketball team is not the one with the star player who makes all the baskets. It's the one whose players pass the ball, and help each other to make the right plays.

## Research Activities

Throughout the unit, you will learn about what can get done when people work as a team. Do some research. Find out about a team that worked together to accomplish something important. Write about the team. What did they accomplish? How did they work together to accomplish their goal?

# Keep Track of Ideas

As you read, keep track of the teams that you are learning about. Use a Chart Foldable to keep track of all your information. At the top of the left column, write Our Teams. On each fold, write what you learn each week about family teams, animal teams, community teams, and work teams.

| Unit Theme | Week 1 | Week 2 | Week 3 | Week 4 | Week 5 |
|------------|--------|--------|--------|--------|--------|
|            |        |        |        |        |        |

## Research Toolkit

### Conduct Your Unit 4 Research Online with:

#### Research Roadmap
Follow step-by-step guide to complete your research project.

#### Online Resources
- Topic Finder and other Research Tools
- Videos and Virtual Fieldtrips
- Photos and Drawings for Presentations
- Related Articles and Web Resources

#### California Web Site Links
 Go to **www.macmillanmh.com** for more information.

### California People

**Jackie Robinson, Baseball Player**
Jackie Robinson was raised in Southern California and attended the University of California at Los Angeles (UCLA).

# WORKING AS ONE

## Talk About It

People with different strengths work together in teams. What strengths do you bring to a team?

LOG ON Find out more about working as one at **www.macmillanmh.com**.

# Vocabulary

| | |
|---|---|
| beamed | fabric |
| argued | purchased |
| possessions | quarreling |

## Dictionary

**Multiple-Meaning Words** are words that have more than one meaning.

Use a dictionary to find the meaning of *beamed* in the first sentence. Remember to look up the base word.

# Community Works

**by Jenna Rabin**

One bright day, as the sunlight **beamed** through the windows, Mr. Turner's class started to plan the third-grade community service project.

"Okay," said Mr. Turner. "Let's share some ideas and listen to each other."

A few students raised their hands. Mr. Turner called on Mark. "We could clean up the small park—pick up trash and paint the benches," said Mark.

Rachel got annoyed. She **argued** with Mark. "You just want that park clean for yourself. Everyone else uses the big park across town. I think we should serve meals at the homeless shelter."

"Now, Rachel. Everyone should have a chance to share his or her ideas. It's okay to disagree, but we should still treat each other nicely."

"Sorry, Mr. Turner," Rachel said.

Jen cut in, "There are people who don't have many **possessions**, not even warm clothing. We could collect **fabric** for making nice, warm clothes for them!"

Cara added, "I read about a class that raised money and **purchased** notebooks and pencils for kids from a discount store."

"We could do crafts with people in nursing homes or hospitals," said Maria.

"Crafts?" groaned Sameer. "I'm really bad at crafts. I'm all thumbs! But how about a walkathon. I'm a fast walker, and we'd get exercise," he said. This made everyone laugh and stop their **quarreling** over who had the best idea.

Then Mr. Turner spoke. "All of your ideas are great. I'm going to write them on the board. Then we will take a class vote. This way we can choose a community service project that most people want to do."

The students agreed this was a good plan.

## Reread for **Comprehension**

### Make Inferences and Analyze

**Draw Conclusions** Authors sometimes give readers **clues** about characters, setting, and story events. Readers should analyze these clues and **draw conclusions**. You can draw a conclusion about the characters, setting, or events by using story clues and what you already know.

Reread the selection. Use your Conclusion Map to draw a conclusion about Rachel. Use Rachel's actions and reactions as your clues.

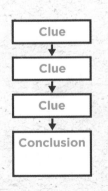

**Comprehension**

### Genre

A **Fable** is a short story that teaches a moral.

### Make Inferences and Analyze

✓ **Draw Conclusions**

As you read, use your Conclusion Map.

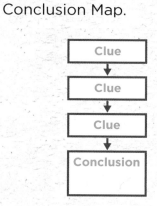

Clue

↓

Clue

↓

Clue

↓

Conclusion

### Read to Find Out

How will the brothers get along at the end of the story?

# Seven Spools of Thread

## A KWANZAA STORY

BY **ANGELA SHELF MEDEARIS**
ILLUSTRATED BY **DANIEL MINTER**

Award
Winning
Selection

11

**In a small African village** in the country of Ghana there lived an old man and his seven sons. After the death of his wife, the old man became both father and mother to the boys. The seven brothers were handsome young men. Their skin was as smooth and dark as the finest mahogany wood. Their limbs were as straight and strong as warriors' spears.

But they were a disappointment to their father. From morning until night, the family's small home was filled with the sound of the brothers' **quarreling**.

As soon as the sun brought forth a new day, the brothers began to argue. They **argued** all morning about how to tend the crops. They argued all afternoon about the weather.

"It is hot," said the middle son.

"No—a cool breeze is blowing!" said the second son.

They argued all evening about when to return home.

"It will be dark soon," the youngest said. "Let's finish this row and begin anew tomorrow."

"No, it's too early to stop," called the third son.

"Can't you see the sun is setting?" shouted the sixth son.

And so it would continue until the moon **beamed** down and the stars twinkled in the sky.

At mealtime, the young men argued until the stew was cold and the fu fu was hard.

"You gave him more than you gave me," whined the third son.

"I divided the food equally," said their father.

"I will starve with only this small portion on my plate," complained the youngest.

"If you don't want it, I'll eat it!" said the oldest son. He grabbed a handful of meat from his brother's plate.

"Stop being so greedy!" said the youngest.

And so it went on every night. It was often morning before the seven brothers finished dinner.

One sad day, the old man died and was buried. At sunrise the next morning, the village Chief called the brothers before him.

"Your father has left an inheritance," said the Chief.

The brothers whispered excitedly among themselves.

"I know my father left me everything because I am the oldest son," said the oldest.

"I know my father left me everything because I am the youngest son," said the youngest.

"He left everything to me," said the middle son. "I know I was his favorite."

"Eeeh!" said the second son. "Everything is mine!"

The brothers began shouting and shoving. Soon, all seven were rolling around on the ground, hitting and kicking each other.

"Stop that this instant!" the Chief shouted.

The brothers stopped fighting. They shook the dust off their clothes and sat before the Chief, eyeing each other suspiciously.

"Your father has decreed that all of his property and **possessions** will be divided among you equally," said the Chief. "But first, by the time the moon rises tonight, you must learn how to make gold out of these spools of silk thread. If you do not, you will be turned out of your home as beggars."

The oldest brother received blue thread. The next brother, red. The next, yellow. The middle son was given orange thread; the next, green; the next, black; and the youngest son received white thread. For once, the brothers were speechless.

The Chief spoke again. "From this moment forward, you must not argue among yourselves or raise your hands in anger towards one another. If you do, your father's property and all his possessions will be divided equally among the poorest of the villagers. Go quickly; you only have a little time."

The brothers bowed to the Chief and hurried away.

> **Draw Conclusions**
> Why were the brothers speechless after listening to the Chief?

When the seven Ashanti brothers arrived at their farm, something unusual happened. They sat side by side, from the oldest to the youngest, without saying anything unkind to each other.

"My brothers," the oldest said after a while, "let us shake hands and make peace among ourselves."

"Let us never argue or fight again," said the youngest brother.

The brothers placed their hands together and held each other tightly.

For the first time in years, peace rested within the walls of their home.

"My brothers," said the third son quietly, "surely our father would not turn us into the world as beggars."

"I agree," said the middle son. "I do not believe our father would have given us the task of turning thread into gold if it were impossible."

"Could it be," said the oldest son, "that there might be small pieces of gold in this thread?"

The sun beamed hotly overhead. Yellow streams of light crept inside the hut. Each brother held up his spool of thread. The beautiful colors sparkled in the sunlight. But there were no nuggets of gold in these spools.

"I'm afraid not, my brother," said the sixth son. "But that was a good idea."

"Thank you, my brother," said the oldest.

"Could it be," said the youngest, "that by making something from this thread we could earn a fortune in gold?"

"Perhaps," said the oldest, "we could make cloth out of this thread and sell it. I believe we can do it."

"This is a good plan," said the middle son. "But we do not have enough of any one color to make a full bolt of cloth."

"What if," said the third son, "we weave the thread together to make a cloth of many colors?"

"But our people do not wear cloth like that," said the fifth son. "We wear only cloth of one color."

"Maybe," said the second, "we could make a cloth that is so special, everyone will want to wear it."

"My brothers," said the sixth son, "we could finish faster if we all worked together."

"I know we can succeed," said the middle son.

The seven Ashanti brothers went to work. Together they cut the wood to make a loom. The younger brothers held the pieces together while the older brothers assembled the loom.

They took turns weaving cloth out of their spools of thread. They made a pattern of stripes and shapes that looked like the wings of birds. They used all the colors— blue, red, yellow, orange, green, black, and white. Soon the brothers had several pieces of beautiful multicolored cloth.

When the cloth was finished, the seven brothers took turns neatly folding the brightly colored **fabric**. Then they placed it into seven baskets and put the baskets on their heads.

The brothers formed a line from the oldest to the youngest and began the journey to the village. The sun slowly made a golden path across the sky. The brothers hurried down the long, dusty road as quickly as they could.

As soon as they entered the marketplace, the seven Ashanti brothers called out, "Come and buy the most wonderful cloth in the world! Come and buy the most wonderful cloth in the world!"

They unfolded a bolt and held it up for all to see. The multicolored fabric glistened like a rainbow. A crowd gathered around the seven Ashanti brothers.

"Oh," said one villager. "I have never seen cloth so beautiful! Look at the unusual pattern!"

"Ah," said another. "This is the finest fabric in all the land! Feel the texture!"

**Draw Conclusions**
What have the brothers learned?

The brothers smiled proudly. Suddenly, a man dressed in magnificent robes pushed his way to the front of the crowd. Everyone stepped back respectfully. It was the King's treasurer. He rubbed the cloth between the palms of his hands. Then he held it up to the sunlight.

"What a thing of beauty," he said, fingering the material. "This cloth will make a wonderful gift for the King! I must have all of it."

The seven brothers whispered together.

"Cloth fit for a king," said the oldest, "should be **purchased** at a price only a king can pay. It is yours for one bag of gold."

"Sold," said the King's treasurer. He untied his bag of gold and spilled out many pieces for the brothers.

The seven Ashanti brothers ran out of the marketplace and back down the road to their village.

A shining silver moon began to creep up in the sky. Panting and dripping with sweat, the brothers threw themselves before the Chief's hut.

"Oh, Chief," said the oldest, "we have turned the thread into gold!"

The Chief came out of his hut and sat upon a stool.

The oldest brother poured the gold out onto the ground.

"Have you argued or fought today?" asked the Chief.

"No, my Chief," said the youngest. "We have been too busy working together to argue or fight."

"Then you have learned the lesson your father sought to teach you," said the Chief. "All that he had is now yours."

The older brothers smiled happily, but the youngest son looked sad.

"What about the poor people in the village?" he asked. "We receive an inheritance, but what will they do?"

"Perhaps," said the oldest, "we can teach them how to turn thread into gold."

The Chief smiled. "You have learned your lesson very well."

The seven Ashanti brothers taught their people carefully. The village became famous for its beautiful, multicolored cloth, and the villagers prospered.

From that day until this, the seven Ashanti brothers have worked together, farming the land.

And they have worked peacefully, in honor of their father.

*Sticks in a bundle are unbreakable.*
*—African Proverb*

# WEAVING A TALE WITH ANGELA AND DANIEL

Author **Angela Shelf Medearis** wrote this story to celebrate the African American holiday Kwanzaa. When Angela was growing up, there were no books for her to read about her African American heritage. Today she writes books about African Americans so readers can feel proud of who they are.

Illustrator **Daniel Minter** often carves and paints on wood, just as he did for this story. Woodcarving is an important part of traditional African art. Daniel's carvings help keep these traditional arts alive.

**Other books** by Angela Shelf Medearis: *Too Much Talk* and *The Freedom Riddle*

 **LOG ON** Find out more about Angela Shelf Medearis and Daniel Minter at **www.macmillanmh.com**.

**CA Author's Purpose**
Did Angela Shelf Medearis write this story to inform or entertain? What clues tell you her purpose for writing?

# CA Critical Thinking

## Summarize

Summarize the plot of *Seven Spools of Thread*. Use your Conclusion Map to help you recall clues that tell how the brothers behave at the end.

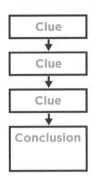

| Clue |
| --- |
| Clue |
| Clue |
| Conclusion |

## Think and Compare

1. The Chief orders the brothers to make gold from thread. How is this different from ordering them to stop **quarreling**? **Draw a conclusion** about the Chief's character based on his actions. **Make Inferences and Analyze: Draw Conclusions**

2. Look back at pages 21–23. What lesson about teamwork do the brothers learn? Use story details in your answer. **Analyze**

3. Think of a time you had to work with a friend or family member. What did you learn from your experience? **Apply**

4. The brothers teach the villagers how to weave the special cloth. Why is this better than giving the villagers money? Explain. **Evaluate**

5. Reread "Community Works" on pages 8–9. How is the problem in that story similar to the problem in *Seven Spools of Thread*? How are the solutions to the problems different? Use details from both stories to support your answer. **Reading/Writing Across Texts**

## Science

**Genre**

**Nonfiction** Some articles give the reader information about people, places, things, or events.

✓ **Text Feature**

**Rules** are a list of ways you should behave.

**Content Vocabulary**

sphere

rotates

axis

# WHAT CAUSES DAY AND NIGHT?

### by Keisha Oliver

Believe it or not, people used to think that Earth stood still while the sun traveled around it each day. It is simple to see why they thought this. The sun rises in the morning, moves across the sky, and disappears at night. Today we know much more about the movement of the sun and Earth.

The movement of Earth causes day and night. Earth is shaped like a ball, or **sphere**. As Earth **rotates**, or turns, there is daylight where Earth faces the sun. There is darkness where Earth is turned away from the sun.

Earth is rotating all the time, but we do not feel it. It takes 24 hours for Earth to make one full rotation. This rotation is equal to one day.

## RULES FOR DAYTIME AND NIGHTTIME

**Reading Rules**

Follow these rules to help you stay safe when you are outside in the daytime or the nighttime.

**Daytime Rules**

1. Do not look directly at the sun.
2. Wear sunglasses when outside in daylight.
3. Wear sunscreen.

**Nighttime Rules**

1. Wear bright clothing so you can be seen.
2. Make sure you tell a responsible adult where you are at all times.

# EARTH MOVES!

Earth rotates around an imaginary line called an **axis**. The axis is drawn through the center of Earth. The equator is a name for the imaginary circle that goes around the middle of Earth.

Since Earth is tilted toward or away from the sun, the amount of heat and energy changes at different places. The temperature is warmer at the equator and colder at the two poles. Earth's tilt also changes the amount of light found in different places at different times of the year. This is why night can last for months in Alaska!

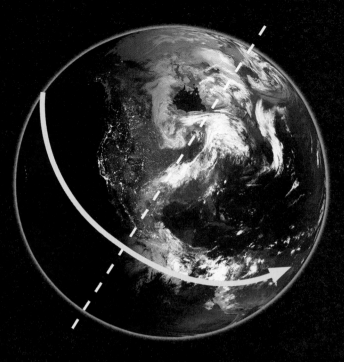

**As Earth moves around the sun, it turns on its axis. Places near the equator receive nearly the same amount of sunlight all year long.**

 **Critical Thinking**

1. Look at the diagram above. Describe Earth's axis. **Reading a Diagram**

2. How long does it take Earth to make a complete rotation? Describe how this rotation affects daylight. **Recall**

3. Why is the sun important in *Seven Spools of Thread*? **Reading/Writing Across Texts**

 **Science Activity**

Research two areas of Earth with different temperatures. Write a paragraph summarizing your research. Draw a diagram to explain how the tilt of Earth on its axis affects the temperatures in the areas you researched.

 Find out more about day and night at **www.macmillanmh.com**.

35

### ✔ Dialogue

Dialogue is what characters say to one another. Dialogue helps the reader know what is happening in the story.

# Reading and Writing Connection

Read the passage below. Notice how author Angela Shelf Medearis integrates dialogue to show what is happening in the story.

**An excerpt from**
*Seven Spools of Thread*

The author uses dialogue to show that the characters are arguing.

They argued all morning about how to tend the crops. They argued all afternoon about the weather.

"It is hot," said the middle son.

"No—a cool breeze is blowing!" said the second son.

They argued all evening about when to return home.

"It will be dark soon," the youngest said. "Let's finish this row and begin anew tomorrow."

"No, it's too early to stop," called the third son.

"Can't you see the sun is setting?" shouted the sixth son.

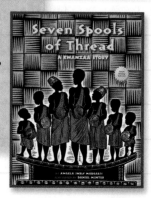

# Read and Find

Read about Will's experience below. How did he use dialogue to show what was happening? Use the Writer's Checklist to help you.

## Zebra Print Pants?

### By Will S.

"I can't believe you're wearing that!" sighed Mom.

"What? I'm comfortable!" my dad replied.

"I will not be seen with you in those zebra-print pants!" Dad looked funny.

"You'll have to go with someone else to Bob's party," Dad said.

Just like that, Mom said, "All right, Will let's get going!" I rolled my eyes.

Read about my well-dressed family.

## Writer's Checklist

✔ Did the author make clear who was speaking?

✔ Does the author show what is happening through the characters' dialogue?

☑ Does it feel as if you are listening to people talking as you read?

# Unique Talents

**CA** **Talk About It**

What are some unique talents of people you know?

**LOG ON** ▶ Find out more about unique talents at www.macmillanmh.com.

39

# The Choir Contest

Valley School and Union School competed against each other in everything. When both schools wanted to help raise money for the volunteer fire departments in their county, the students at Valley decided to put on a concert. When the students at Union heard about Valley's plans, Union students suggested they have a contest: which school choir could raise the most money? A local contest would help to **guarantee** that many people would come.

The students **pleaded** with their choir teachers to help. The teachers agreed because the contest was for a good cause.

Both schools hurried to choose songs and make costumes. Worn out and **exhausted** from all the **preparations**, many singers at Valley became sick. They feared they would have to cancel the concert. Then the choir teacher from Union had an idea. "What if we combine the best of both our concerts for one big concert?" she asked her students.

Everyone loved the idea. On show night, people from all over the county attended the concert. The audience loved the music and the **brilliance** of the costumes. Not only did the two rival schools raise money, but they also learned to work together. Everyone in the county felt **affection** for these two schools and applauded the work they accomplished together.

## Reread for **Comprehension**

### Evaluate

**Theme**

The **theme** is the main message that the author wants to get across to the reader. Knowing the theme can help you evaluate what is important and meaningful in the story. Reread the story to find the theme. Use your Theme Map to identify **clues** to the story's theme by telling about characters, setting, and plot.

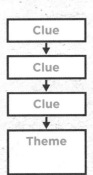

Clue
↓
Clue
↓
Clue
↓
Theme

**Comprehension**

### Genre

A **Folktale** is a story that is passed from person to person in a culture. Folktales usually use animals that dress and act like humans. Folktales teach a lesson.

### Evaluate

**Theme**

As you read, use your Theme Map.

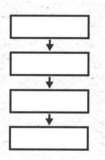

### Read to Find Out

How does Nacho help his new family find their way home?

# NACHO and LOLITA

by Pam Muñoz Ryan

illustrated by Claudia Rueda

Award Winning Author

Once, when the two Californias ran *alto y baja*, high and low along the sea of the Pacific, a mysterious bird landed on the branch of a mesquite tree in the valley of San Juan. His name was Nacho and he was a *pitacoche*. Rare and majestic, he heralded the sunset with whistling songs and carried the colors of the world in his feathers.

From his perch on the edge of the churchyard, Nacho, could see the panorama. Acres of dirt rolled into thirsty riverbeds that held only a trickle of water. Nothing grew in the fields. Even the leaves of the mesquite tree matched the adobe of the Mission San Juan Capistrano.

What a dismal place, Nacho thought.

Everything seemed to blend into the same brown landscape…

…except for Nacho.

With a little too much pride, he spread his feathers, preening and fluffing as he waited for the day to fade. Then, at the moment the sun closed its eye, Nacho trumpeted the passing of the light with song, his trill like a mysterious wind.

"OO EEE AHH OOO EEEE OOOO."

A crowd gathered to admire his evening ritual. "He is so beautiful and his call is so haunting. He must be a spirit from the past," someone whispered.

"Or a prophet of the future," said another.

Nacho knew the truth. He was the only *pitacoche* for thousands of miles and hundreds of years. His **brilliance** sometimes brought him attention. But what good was it when he had no other bird with whom to share his joy?

**Theme**
Why don't Nacho's brilliant feathers and voice bring him joy?

The busy churchyard was a pleasant change from Nacho's lonesome travels. He watched people prepare for the March feast of St. Joseph. He listened to the talk about the return of *las golondrinas*, the swallows, and the more he heard, the more curious he became.

"It is a miracle," said one man. "Every year the tiny birds cross the great waters to this very place, arriving on the feast day. Then, when the days grow shorter, they leave again for another world, always together. *¡Una familia fantástica!*"

How romantic, thought Nacho.

The swallows were everything he was not. They were small and strong. He was big and bound to the land, unable to fly long distances without resting. They were a fantastic family flying together over the ocean. He didn't belong to anyone.

Intrigued by the people's **preparations** and caught up in their enthusiasm, Nacho wondered what *he* could do to help.

I have nothing to offer, he thought, except my songs.

On the feast day, Nacho woke to the clanging of bells. People ran into the churchyard and pointed skyward.

"*¡Las golondrinas!*" they cried.

A scout swallow circled above, then another, followed by a flight of swallows trailing in the sky. All morning they came, swooping down toward the mission and landing in the eaves.

One small swallow chose the belfry of the chapel to make her nest. All day, she flew back and forth to the riverbed, gathering bits of mud and twigs. Each time she passed Nacho, she peeked at him.

Did she notice my glorious feathers? he wondered. My regal stature? I *am* colorful and noble. Or was it something else? Could she see my pitiful and lonely spirit?

As the small swallow made her last trip of the day, the sun said good night and Nacho began *un arullo*, a lullaby.

Every swallow leaned forward to hear the magnificent serenade. The small one stopped on the ox cart and listened.

When Nacho finished his song, he plucked one of his feathers and flew to the ox cart. As was his destiny, once a colorful feather was spent, a gray feather grew back in its place. But Nacho didn't mind. When the swallow took it in her beak, by the mystery of the ages, it became a blue hibiscus.

"What is your name?" Nacho asked.

"Lolita," she said, her cheeks flushing the faintest pink.

"LOOOOOWWW-LEEEEEE-TAHHH."

He repeated, and his voice filled with notes he had never dreamed of singing.

Days passed and Nacho cheerfully busied himself among the swallows.

He carried bits of dry grass and dollops of mud to their nests, especially Lolita's.

After the speckled eggs appeared, he used his wide wings to protect them, especially Lolita's.

When the chicks were born, he searched for beetles, flies, and spiders, and delivered them to each home, especially Lolita's.

"Thank you, Nacho," she said. "You are splendid. You are magnificent!"

Nacho's bright feathers fluffed, and his heart felt as cozy as the warming breezes.

Every evening, his lullaby echoed throughout the mission.

"LOW-LEEEEE-TAH, OOO EEEE OOOO."

By summertime, Lolita and her chicks were always by Nacho's side. Nacho was so full with **affection** and purpose that he could not remember a time before he came to the mission.

Together, he and Lolita watched the chicks fledge and fly. As the days grew longer, they stayed in the fields until sunset, foraging for worms and bugs.

Then one day a September gust brought a message with the wind, and a hint of uneasiness settled among the swallows.

"I'm afraid we must leave soon," Lolita reminded him. "And now there is talk that we will never come back here again. The water is drying up. We need mud to make our nests. We need flowers and trees to attract insects, so there will be enough food. Without the river to guide us, we will easily miss this spot next year."

Nacho panicked. He'd forgotten that Lolita would have to leave. Now she might never return.

"Stay with me," he **pleaded**.

"It's too cold here in the winter. I must migrate or I will die. You come with me," she begged. "You would love it in the south Americas. Rivers overflow the banks, flowers decorate the fields …" Lolita looked toward the ocean, as if she couldn't wait to cross it, "…and the sunsets are the color of papayas."

Nacho hung his head. "I can't fly that far," he said sadly. "I am too big."

"I've asked the others," said Lolita. "There is one idea that might work, if you are willing."

Lolita led Nacho to a quiet cove.

"Carry this branch in your talons," she said. "Fly as long as you can. When you grow tired, drop the branch into the water and rest on it. Then wait for your strength to return so you can fly again."

Nacho did as Lolita instructed and bobbed safely on the calm water.

He practiced every day until the October morning when the scout swallows left and the others prepared to follow.

Could he really go with them? Just the chance made him feel as if he could fly forever.

At last, the time had come to leave the mission. Nacho and Lolita hurried to a cliff's edge, facing the vast ocean. Nacho gripped the branch. The breeze lifted him and he followed Lolita over the rough open sea. But after a very short distance, Nacho was **exhausted**. He dropped the branch and landed on it just as he'd practiced. Lolita circled above, waiting for him.

Before Nacho was ready to fly again, choppy waves rocked him from his perch.

He splashed and struggled and began to sink.

"Nacho! Nacho!" cried Lolita.

He slipped farther and farther beneath the swells.

A thousand swallows turned back, flew down, and lifted Nacho to safety.

On the clifftop, gasping for air, he knew the truth. A big *pitacoche* and a small swallow were not meant to be together.

"Go," he told Lolita. "We will meet in our dreams."

When she disappeared from sight, his heart felt as barren as the land.

That night as the sun slid away, Nacho's song ached with sadness.

"LOW-LEEEEE-TAH, I LOOOOVE YOU!"

Winter came with heavy fog. Nacho sat sentry in the mesquite tree and remembered the happy times with *la familia fantástica.*

He thought about the first time he saw Lolita and how he had given her one of his feathers. He looked at the gray feather that had grown back in its place. I would give all of my colorful feathers if the swallows and my Lolita would come back, he thought. Wasn't there some way to **guarantee** their return?

Nacho flew to the belfry every day. The blue hibiscus had taken root among the mud nests and even though the flowers were gone, the strong vine wove its way through the tower, exactly as Lolita had done to his heart.

When spring poked its head into February, the vine held buds that promised returning blossoms. All that from one feather.

Suddenly, Nacho knew what he must do.

In March, when the people began their preparations for the feast of St. Joseph, Nacho began to prepare, too. He flew to the fields, plucked his orange and yellow feathers, and as fast as he planted them, the acres bloomed with poppies and mustard. He left a trail of blue feathers in the riverbed and it overflowed, filling the small creeks and marshes. He pushed green feathers into the soil until palms danced in the breeze and orange trees flourished. He tucked feathers over arches and balconies, and draperies of bougainvillea appeared.

As Nacho worked, he wondered if the swallows would find their way. Determined, he planted feathers in every patch of earth in the churchyard until a splendor burst forth.

Nacho had used every feather, except one.

When the hallowed bells rang as if they'd never rung before, Nacho searched the sky for Lolita. A million thoughts raced through his mind. What if she doesn't recognize me? What if she doesn't like me now that I'm as drab as a mud hen?

**Theme**
What does Nacho do with his feathers? Why is this important?

Nacho watched the scout swallows dive around the mission in a frenzy of joy and excitement. One after another they came, followed by a flurry of swallows. He turned his head toward the heavens and waited.

When at last Lolita found Nacho in the mesquite tree, it was as if they'd been together for thousands of miles and hundreds of years.

"I no longer have my beautiful colors," he said.

"To me, you will always be splendid," she said.

Together, they flew toward the river to gather mud and twigs to make a nest.

Before the day faded, Nacho plucked the last bright feather from his wing and tossed it toward the westward clouds.

Then, at the moment the sun closed its eye, Nacho heralded the passing of the day with a concert…

...against a papaya sky.

# TEAM UP
## with Pam and Claudia

**Pam Muñoz Ryan** spent many long, hot summers as a child riding her bike to the library in California's San Joaquin Valley. She loved the library because her family didn't have a swimming pool, and the library was air-conditioned. Now Pam focuses her energy and her vivid imagination on writing children's books.

**Claudia Rueda** went to college at the University of California, Berkeley, in San Francisco where she learned how to illustrate children's books. She has published books in the United States, Spain, and Mexico.

**Other books** by Pam Muñoz Ryan: *Mice and Beans and When Marian Sang*

**LOG ON** Find out more about Pam Muñoz Ryan and Claudia Rueda at **www.macmillanmh.com.**

 **Author's Purpose**

What was Pam Muñoz Ryan's purpose for writing this story? How do you know?

# CA Critical Thinking

## Summarize

Use your Theme Map to help you summarize *Nacho and Lolita.* Tell about the setting, characters, and events.

| Clue |
|------|
| ↓ |
| Clue |
| ↓ |
| Clue |
| ↓ |
| Theme |

## Think and Compare

1. Use your Theme Map to identify the **theme** of *Nacho and Lolita.* What story details tell about the theme? Evaluate: **Theme**

2. Reread pages 49–55. How has Nacho changed after caring for Lolita and her chicks? **Analyze**

3. In what ways are pitacoches the same as swallows? How are they different? **Evaluate**

4. What **preparations** are done in your community to get ready for a new season? **Apply**

5. Reread "The Choir Contest" on pages 40–41. How does the community in that passage find a solution to a problem? How is it similar to Nacho's solution to the problem in this selection? **Reading/Writing Across Texts**

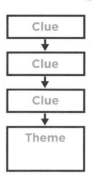

# Haiku

## Poetry

A **Haiku** is a form of poetry that usually describes a moment or scene in nature using just three lines. The first and third lines often have five syllables each, and the second line often has seven.

## Literary Elements

**Consonance** is a repetition of similar consonant sounds, especially at the ends of two or more words.

A **metaphor** compares two different things without using *like* or *as*.

Calling an umbrella a "tent" is an example of a metaphor.

Broken and broken
Again on the sea, the moon
So easily mends.

—*Chosu*

Shiny colored tents
Pop up above people's heads
At the first raindrop.

—*Myra Cohn Livingston*

64

*Hops, prints,* and *sets*
all end with the same sound
to create consonance.

A lonely sparrow
Hops upon the snow and prints
Sets of maple leaves.
—*Kazue Mizumura*

## (CA) Critical Thinking

1. What is the metaphor in Kazue Mizumura's haiku? What two things are being compared? **Metaphor**

2. What details does Myra Cohn Livingston use in her haiku? How do they help you picture what is happening? **Evaluate**

3. In *Nacho and Lolita*, Nacho helps make the world a more beautiful place. How do these haiku make the objects they describe more beautiful as well? **Reading/Writing Across Texts**

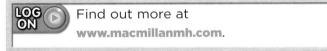

LOG ON ▶ Find out more at **www.macmillanmh.com**.

CA **Writing**

✓ **Dialogue**

Instead of using telling sentences, you can use dialogue to let readers know what is happening in a story.

Read the passage below. Notice how author Pam Muñoz Ryan integrates dialogue to show what is happening in the story.

**An excerpt from**
*Nacho and Lolita*

The author shows what the characters believe about *Nacho* by showing what they said. The dialogue helps us imagine what the moment sounded like instead of just what it looked like.

Then, at the moment the sun closed its eye, Nacho trumpeted the passing of the light with song, his trill like a mysterious wind.

"OO EEE AHH OOO EEEE OOOO."

A crowd gathered to admire his evening ritual. "He is so beautiful and his call is so haunting. He must be a spirit from the past," someone whispered.

"Or a prophet of the future," said another.

66

# Read and Find

How did Tess use dialogue to show what was happening? Use the Writer's Checklist below.

# Lunchtime

### By Tess M.

"What is that?" I asked Justin.

"What do you mean? It's my lunch!" Justin replied.

"I can't believe you are going to eat that soggy brown and red mess!"

"My sister sat on my sandwich on the bus!" Justin looked embarrassed.

"I wouldn't eat that." I said . I was still upset about this morning.

Read about what happened at lunch today.

# Writer's Checklist

☑ Did the author use dialogue instead of telling statements?

☑ Does the author show what is happening through what the characters say?

☑ Does the dialogue help you know how the characters are feeling?

Why is it a good idea for people to work with others to solve problems?

LOG ON ▷ Find out more about community teamwork at **www.macmillanmh.com**.

# Community TEAMWORK

# A Higher GOAL

This girl plays soccer in Kibera, a slum in Nairobi.

Kibera's kids play hard, even after hours of cleanup. In one year, the kids will usually clear more than 250 tons of garbage from Kibera.

It is game day in Nairobi, Kenya. Hundreds of kids gather at a soccer field in Kibera (ky-bee-rah). Before kickoff, the kids grab hold of spades and rakes. They push wheelbarrows and fill trash bags. They happily spend five hours clearing trash and sorting recycling.

That may sound like a strange warm-up to you. But digging into Kibera's mountains of trash is the only way players can earn a spot on a soccer team.

Kibera is a crowded city. The tightly packed in residents are poor. Many have health problems.

In 2001 a concerned American student named Rye Barcott began Carolina for Kibera (CFK). He wanted Kibera's kids to have a better life. Pregame cleanups help kids "accept some responsibility for the welfare of their community," he told TFK.

The kids in Kibera know that CFK isn't just for kicks. Their cleanups have helped raise **awareness** about **pollution**. The kids have worked together to keep their neighborhoods cleaner and safer. "CFK is much more than soccer," says Barcott.

# Words to Live By

These words were written by two famous people. Their messages have inspired people to help others. They may inspire you to do the same.

"Ask not what your country can do for you— ask what you can do for your country."
—*John F. Kennedy*

"We make a living by what we do, but we make a life by what we give."
—*Winston Churchill*

## Service with a Smile

Here are tips to get you and a group of friends started on a meaningful community service project.

- Identify a problem that exists in your community.

- Learn more. With friends, come up with resourceful ways to solve the problem.

- Set goals and decide what you'll need.

- Get your school involved. Encourage students and parents to help out.

- Have fun. Helping to make a difference should make you feel good. **Emphasize** the good you are doing for the world.

- Spread the word. **Utilize** your local newspaper. Write about what you're doing. Soon, others may hear about your project and decide to pitch in.

LOG ON ▶ Find out more about community projects at **www.macmillanmh.com**.

# A Solution to POLLUTION

California's beautiful beaches may be in danger. People sometimes dump trash on them, leaving the beaches ugly and polluted. The state cannot afford to pick up all the trash. Fortunately, Californians lend a helping hand. Each year 50,000 volunteers grab large garbage bags and rakes. Then they head to the shore for a busy day of work. On this special day, the world's largest garbage collection takes place.

California has many beautiful beaches along its 1,100 miles of coastline.

## Clean Changes

Coastal Cleanup Day is usually held in mid-September, at the end of the beach season and before school starts. There are more than 700 cleanup sites in California. Areas targeted for cleanup are on the coast, in waterways, and around other wildlife areas.

California's day is part of International Coastal Cleanup. All 50 states and over 100 countries participate in this global program to team up to clean up. The program also helps raise **awareness** about coastal **pollution**.

Families, service groups, students, and neighbors join forces for California Coastal Cleanup Day.

## Planting for Change

Buena Park High School is one of many schools that takes part in this event. In 2004 students helped by working in a wildlife refuge. Seal Beach National Wildlife Refuge near San Diego is a huge salt-marsh preserve. Many endangered birds live in this wetland habitat, including California brown pelicans.

Buena Park teens and adult helpers spent four hours working in the wildlife refuge. First, they cleaned up the area. Then, the class planted native plants that would grow naturally in this environment. Native plants are important for wildlife. They provide proper food and habitats for animals and insects that live in the area. The students made sure to **utilize** their knowledge about the marsh to make it safer for the native critters.

## Making Time

Since California Coastal Cleanup started in 1995, more than 750,000 Californians have taken part. Their efforts have helped remove 12 million pounds of trash on the state's coasts and waterways. Worldwide, volunteers have removed 116 million pounds of trash. Each year they promise to remove even more.

Many of the schools that participate in California's Coastal Cleanup sign a Coastal Pledge. The pledge, or promise, asks students to do five activities that will help clean up the environment. The activities **emphasize** working together and having fun.

## Written in the Sand

The California Coastal Commission also holds an Ocean Day Kids' Cleanup each May. While cleaning up the beach, the kids learn about marine life. They learn how pollution harms ocean animals and plants.

Many classrooms pledge to help out throughout the year. One sixth-grade class from Los Angeles picked up trash along the Los Angeles River. A high school in Stockton, California, cleared garbage along a four-mile stretch of beach at Half Moon Bay. Other schools adopted a beach. They keep it clean all year round.

## Sending a Message

At the end of the day, the kid helpers stand together in the sand for a photo. Their bodies spell out a giant message, such as "Protect" or "SOS" (Morse code for "help"). Thousands of kids from San Francisco, Los Angeles, Huntington Beach, and other areas look forward to this day every year.

The students and adults who work together realize the good that comes of their hard work. They know that as a group, they are helping to make a difference in the world.

**The word "protect" and a dolphin are formed by 3,000 kids on a Los Angeles beach.**

**CA Critical Thinking**

1. What **problems** are **solved** by California Coastal Cleanup Day?

2. Why is it a good idea to hold the Coastal Cleanup in the middle of September?

3. How might volunteers feel after helping to clean up a beach?

4. How is the **solution** to the trash problem similar in "A Higher Goal" and in this article?

**Test Strategy**

Think and Search The answer is in more than one place. Keep reading to find the answer.

Delonzo Yurcek (top center) and his brothers and sisters give supplies at a shelter in Kalamazoo, Michigan. "We thought they needed more than backpacks," says Delonzo.

# Kids Helping Kids

Delonzo Yurcek often had no backpack for his first day of school. He and his siblings grew up partly as foster children. There was no money for school supplies. They felt ashamed because they didn't have paper and pencils like the other kids.

"We didn't want anyone else to feel like that," says Delonzo. He and his four brothers and sisters were adopted by the Yurceks in 1998. Ann and Jim Yurcek also have six children of their own.

In 2002 the Yurcek family started Backpacks for Kids. The family raised money through garage sales and collecting cans and bottles. The kids also asked neighbors for pencils, paper, and other school supplies. The items were put into backpacks and given to needy kids who couldn't afford the supplies.

That first year, the Yurcek family gave out more than 300 backpacks. Since 2002, Backpacks for Kids has helped 3,000 kids get ready to learn.

**Go on** ▶

**Directions: Now answer Numbers 1–5. Base your answers on the article "Kids Helping Kids."**

1. **Why did Delonzo and his brothers and sisters feel ashamed on the first day of school?**

   A   They didn't have new school clothes like other kids.
   B   They were the only foster children at their school.
   C   They had no money to pay for school lunches.
   D   They didn't have school supplies like other kids.

2. **Why did the Yurcek family start Backpacks for Kids?**

   A   to make new backpacks to give away to foster children
   B   to make sure kids have backpacks and school supplies
   C   to buy backpacks by selling school supplies
   D   to buy school supplies by selling backpacks

   **Tip**
   Look for information in more than one place.

3. **Which of the following is NOT something the Yurcek family did to raise money?**

   A   Have a bake sale.
   B   Go to the neighbors.
   C   Have a garage sale.
   D   Collect bottles and cans.

4. **Has Backpacks for Kids been successful? How can you tell? Use DETAILS from the article to support your answer.**

5. **Backpacks for Kids shows that one family can make a big difference in a community. Do you agree or disagree with this statement? Explain your answer. Use DETAILS from the article.**

# ✏️ Write on Demand

**CA**

Sometimes amazing things happen to people.

Think about an amazing thing that could happen to you.

Now <u>write about</u> this amazing thing.

> Narrative writing tells a story about a personal or fictional experience.

> To figure out if a prompt asks for narrative writing, look for clue words, such as <u>write about</u> and <u>write a story</u>.

Below see how one student begins a response to the prompt above.

> The beginning of the story explains the setting, or where the story takes place.

Today was the big day! I volunteered to talk about our school fundraising project on TV. I entered the studio ready for my big TV break.

First, I answered questions. Then I said, "We need to educate people about the needs in their communities. Local shelters should be stocked for emergencies. It takes time and money."

At the end, the host said, "Someone is here who can help you." Suddenly, the President of the United States walked onto the stage. In his hands was a check for two million dollars!

# Writing Prompt

Respond in writing to the prompt below. Write for
10 minutes. Write as much as you can, as well as you can.
Review the hints below before and after you write.

**CA**

People sometimes have unusual days.

Think about how a day could be unusual.

Now write a short story about an unusual day.

## Writing Hints for Prompts

☑ Read the prompt carefully.

☑ Plan your writing by organizing ideas.

☑ Support your ideas telling more about each event.

☑ Make sure your story has a beginning, middle, and ending.

☑ Review and edit your writing.

☑ Make sure you punctuate dialogue correctly.

**CA** **Talk About It**

How do you and your
family work as a team?

**LOG ON** ▶ Find out more about
cooking at
www.macmillanmh.com.

# Family Teams

# BEN'S BRIGHT IDEA

Dario awoke feeling nervous and **anxious**. He felt **cross** with his teacher, who put him in charge of raising money for the pet shelter. He knew nothing about money or shelters! When Mrs. Scanlon said the class was going to be doing community service, he figured he'd get to sweep the playground. Now he just felt **alarmed** and scared at the thought of having so much responsibility.

There was nothing else to do but search for his older brother, Ben, and ask him for help. **Unfortunately**, the two of them didn't get along, but Ben was very handy. He had **managed** his class fair last year. Dario was feeling desperate. He had to have an idea by Monday, and it was already Friday.

Dario found Ben eating as usual. Just the sight of Ben doing his usual thing was reassuring. Dario felt better already. "Ben, I need to raise some money for the pet shelter. You got any ideas?"

Instead of laughing at him, Ben actually was eager to help. "How about we hold a garage sale? We have lots of old toys and clothes we could sell."

"WOW!" Dario was thrilled. They could **pretend** they had their own business! Big brothers weren't so bad after all.

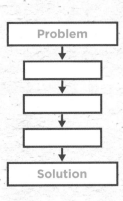

## Reread for **Comprehension**

### ✔ Make Inferences and Analyze

**Problem and Solution** Sometimes, a story's plot begins with a character who has a **problem**. The problem is what the character wants to do, find out, or change. The **solution** is how the problem is solved. A Problem and Solution Chart can help you analyze how the story is organized. Reread the selection to find the problem and how the characters found the solution.

Problem

↓

↓

↓

↓

Solution

**Genre**

**Humor** A humorous story is written to make readers laugh.

**Make Inferences and Analyze**

**Problem and Solution**
As you read, use your Problem and Solution Chart.

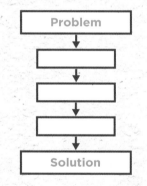

| Problem |
|:---:|

↓

↓

↓

| Solution |
|:---:|

**Read to Find Out**

What does Ramona do about her family's problem?

84

# RAMONA
## AND HER
# FATHER

By Beverly Cleary
illustrated by Ilene Richard

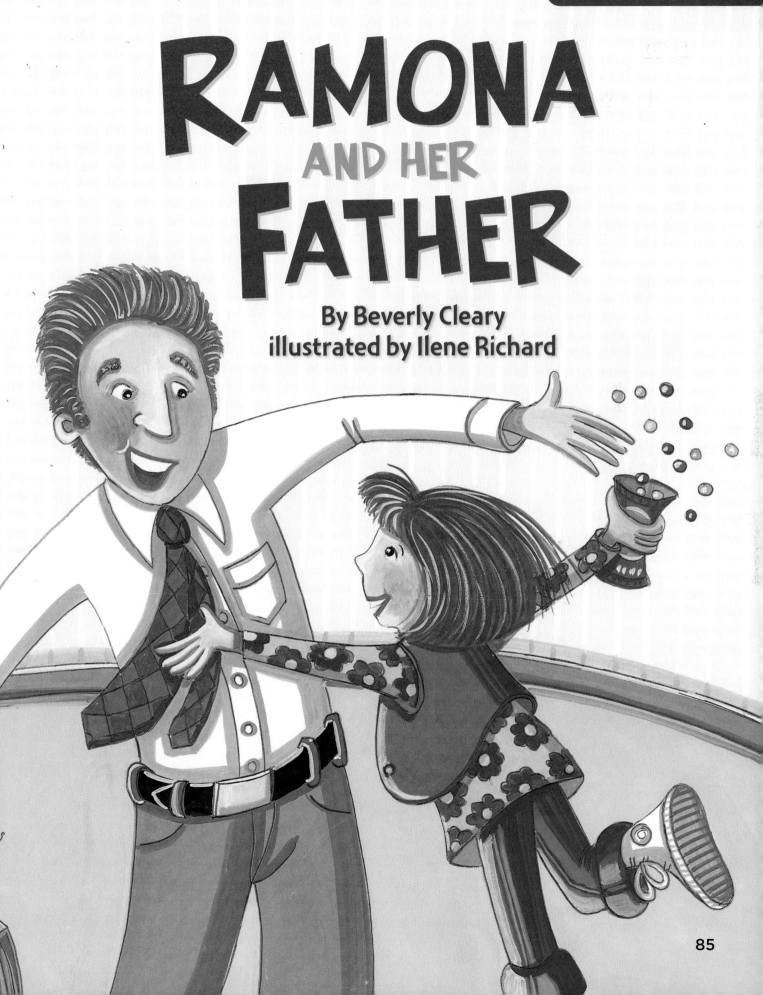

"Something is wrong. Something awful," whispered Beezus. "I can tell by the way they are talking."

Beezus looked so frightened that Ramona became frightened, too. What could be wrong? She tried to think what she might have done to make her parents whisper this way, but she had stayed out of trouble lately. She could not think of a single thing that could be wrong. This frightened her even more. She no longer felt like eating chewy little bears. She wanted to know why her mother and father were whispering in a way that **alarmed** Beezus.

Finally the girls heard her father say in a normal voice, "I think I'll take a shower before supper." This remark was reassuring to Ramona.

"What'll we do now?" whispered Beezus. "I'm scared to go out."

Worry and curiosity, however, urged Beezus and Ramona into the hall.

Trying to **pretend** they were not concerned about their family, the girls walked into the kitchen where Mrs. Quimby was removing leftovers from the refrigerator. "I think we'll eat at home after all," she said, looking sad and **anxious**.

Without being asked, Ramona began to deal four place mats around the dining room table, laying them all right side up. When she was **cross** with Beezus, she laid her sister's place mat face down.

Mrs. Quimby looked at the cold creamed cauliflower with distaste, returned it to the refrigerator, and reached for a can of green beans before she noticed her silent and worried daughters watching her for clues as to what might be wrong.

Mrs. Quimby turned and faced Beezus and Ramona. "Girls, you might as well know. Your father has lost his job."

"But he liked his job," said Ramona, regretting the loss of that hamburger and those French fries eaten in the coziness of a booth. She had known her father to change jobs because he had not liked his work, but she had never heard of him losing a job.

"Was he fired?" asked Beezus, shocked at the news.

Mrs. Quimby opened the green beans and dumped them into a saucepan before she explained. "Losing his job was not your father's fault. He worked for a little company. A big company bought the little company and let out most of the people who worked for the little company."

**Problem and Solution**
What is the Quimbys' problem?

"But we won't have enough money." Beezus understood these things better than Ramona.

"Mother works," Ramona reminded her sister.

"Only part time," said Mrs. Quimby. "And we have to make payments to the bank for the new room. That's why I went to work."

"What will we do?" asked Ramona, alarmed at last. Would they go hungry? Would the men from the bank come and tear down the new room if they couldn't pay for it? She had never thought what it might be like to not have enough money—not that the Quimbys ever had money to spare. Although Ramona had often heard her mother say that house payments, car payments, taxes, and groceries seemed to eat up money, Mrs. Quimby somehow **managed** to make their money pay for all they really needed with a little treat now and then besides.

"We will have to manage as best we can until your father finds work," said Mrs. Quimby. "It may not be easy."

"Maybe I could baby-sit," volunteered Beezus.

As she laid out knives and forks, Ramona wondered how she could earn money, too. She could have a lemonade stand in front of the house, except nobody ever bought lemonade but her father and her friend Howie. She thought about pounding rose petals and soaking them in water to make perfume to sell. **Unfortunately**, the perfume she tried to make always smelled like rotten rose petals, and anyway the roses were almost gone.

"And girls," said Mrs. Quimby, lowering her voice as if she was about to share a secret, "you mustn't do anything to annoy your father. He is worried enough right now."

But he remembered to bring gummy-bears, thought Ramona, who never wanted to annoy her father or her mother either, just Beezus, although sometimes,

without even trying, she succeeded in annoying her whole family. Ramona felt sad and somehow lonely, as if she were left out of something important, because her family was in trouble and there was nothing she could do to help. When she had finished setting the table, she returned to the list she had begun, it now seemed, a long time ago. "But what about Christmas?" she asked her mother.

"Right now Christmas is the least of our worries." Mrs. Quimby looked sadder than Ramona had ever seen her look. "Taxes are due in November. And we have to buy groceries and make car payments and a lot of other things."

"Don't we have any money in the bank?" asked Beezus.

"Not much," admitted Mrs. Quimby, "but your father was given two weeks' pay."

Ramona looked at the list she had begun so happily and wondered how much the presents she had listed would cost. Too much, she knew. Mice were free if you knew the right person, the owner of a mother mouse, so she might get some mice.

Slowly Ramona crossed out ginny pig and the other presents she had listed. As she made black lines through each item, she thought about her family. She did not want her father to be worried, her mother sad, or her sister cross. She wanted her whole family, including Picky-picky, to be happy.

Ramona studied her crayons, chose a pinky-red one because it seemed the happiest color, and printed one more item on her Christmas list to make up for all she had crossed out. One happy family. Beside the words she drew four smiling faces and beside them, the face of a yellow cat, also smiling.

Ramona wished she had a million dollars so her father would be fun again. There had been many changes in the Quimby household since Mr. Quimby had lost his job, but the biggest change was in Mr. Quimby himself.

First of all, Mrs. Quimby found a full-time job working for another doctor, which was good news. However, even a second grader could understand that one paycheck would not stretch as far as two paychecks, especially when there was so much talk of taxes, whatever they were. Mrs. Quimby's new

**Problem and Solution**
What does Mrs. Quimby do to help solve the family problem?

job meant that Mr. Quimby had to be home when Ramona returned from school.

Ramona and her father saw a lot of one another. At first she thought having her father to herself for an hour or two every day would be fun, but when she came home, she found him running the vacuum cleaner, filling out job applications, or sitting on the couch, staring into space. He could not take her to the park because he had to stay near the telephone. Someone might call to offer him a job. Ramona grew uneasy. Maybe he was too worried to love her anymore.

One day Ramona came home to find her father in the living room drinking warmed-over coffee and staring at the television set. On the screen a boy a couple of years younger than Ramona was singing:

Forget your pots, forget your pans.

It's not too late to change your plans.

Spend a little, eat a lot,

Big fat burgers, nice and hot

At your nearest Whopperburger!

Ramona watched him open his mouth wide to bite into a fat cheeseburger with lettuce and tomato spilling out of the bun and thought wistfully of the good old days when the family used to go to the restaurant on payday and when her mother used to bring home little treats—stuffed olives, cinnamon buns for Sunday breakfast, a bag of potato chips.

"That kid must be earning a million dollars. He's singing that commercial every time I turn on the television."

A boy Ramona's age earning a million dollars? Ramona was all interest. "How's he earning a million dollars?" she asked. She had often thought of all the things they could do if they had a million dollars, beginning with turning up the thermostat so they wouldn't have to wear sweaters in the house to save fuel oil.

Mr. Quimby explained. "They make a movie of him singing the commercial, and every time the movie is shown on television he gets paid. It all adds up."

Well! This was a new idea to Ramona. She thought it over as she got out her crayons and paper and knelt on a chair at the kitchen table. Singing a song about hamburgers would not be hard to do. She could do it herself. Maybe she could earn a million dollars like that boy so her father would be fun again, and everyone at school would watch her on television and say, "There's Ramona Quimby. She goes to our school." A million dollars would buy a cuckoo clock for every room in the house, her father wouldn't need a job, the family could go to Disneyland....

"Forget your pots, forget your pans," Ramona began to sing, as she drew a picture of a hamburger and stabbed yellow dots across the top of the bun for sesame seeds. With a million dollars the Quimbys could eat in a restaurant every day if they wanted to.

After that Ramona began to watch for children on television commercials. She saw a boy eating bread and margarine when a crown suddenly appeared on his head with a fanfare of music—ta da! She saw a girl who asked, "Mommy, wouldn't it be nice if caramel apples grew on trees?" and another girl who took a bite of cereal said, "It's good, hm-um," and giggled. There was a boy who asked at the end of a weiner commercial, "Dad, how do you tell a boy hot dog from a girl hot dog?" and a girl who tipped her head to one side and said, "Pop-pop-pop," as she listened to her cereal. Children crunched potato chips, chomped on pickles, gnawed at fried chicken. Ramona grew particularly fond of the curly-haired little girl saying to her mother at the zoo, "Look, Mommy, the elephant's legs are wrinkled just like your pantyhose." Ramona could say all those things.

Ramona began to practice. Maybe someone would see her and offer her a million dollars to make a television commercial.

# BEVERLY AND HER FAMILY OF FANS

**Beverly Cleary's** books are found in over twenty countries in fourteen languages. Her books are translated into Spanish, Swedish, Japanese, and more. Television shows and videos based on the Ramona books are popular in the United States. Why? Probably because Beverly Cleary writes characters who are funny, lovable, and clever. Readers see themselves, their own families, and their own neighborhoods in her books. It is not hard to see why Beverly Cleary is clearly an international favorite.

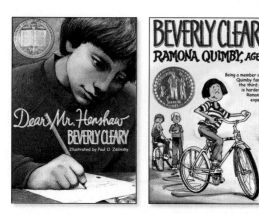

**Other books** by Beverly Cleary: *Dear Mr. Henshaw* and *Ramona Quimby, Age 8*

**CA** **Author's Purpose**
What was Beverly Cleary's purpose for writing this story? How do you know?

LOG ON ▶ Find out more about Beverly Cleary at www.macmillanmh.com.

## CA Critical Thinking

### Summarize

Use your Problem and Solution Chart to summarize
*Ramona and Her Father*. Tell about Ramona's
problem and how she tried to solve it.

| Problem |
|---|
| ↓ |
| |
| ↓ |
| |
| ↓ |
| |
| ↓ |
| Solution |

### Think and Compare

1. Describe two **solutions** Ramona has for helping
   her family with their **problem**. Why might these
   work or not work? **Make Inferences and Analyze:
   Problem and Solution**

2. Reread pages 94–95 of *Ramona and Her Father*. How does
   Ramona change her list, and why? **Analyze**

3. Ramona decides to **pretend** she's an actress in a television
   commercial as acting practice. What is something that you
   have practiced to be good at? **Apply**

4. How have Mr. Quimby's responsibilities changed? Use details
   from the story in your answer. **Evaluate**

5. Read "Ben's Bright Idea" on pages
   82–83. Compare and contrast the
   relationship between the brothers in
   the selection and the relationship
   between the sisters in *Ramona
   and Her Father*. Use details
   from both stories in your answer.
   **Reading/Writing Across Texts**

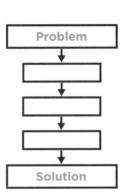

## Poetry

**Free Verse Poems** do not have to follow rhyme schemes but often contain rhythmic patterns and other poetic elements.

### ✔ Literary Elements

The **Speaker** of a poem is the person who is telling the story in the poem.

**Alliteration** is the repetition of the same beginning sound in a series of words.

> The speaker of the poem is a boy, remembering his grandmother.

> "Chat" and "Chairs" are examples of alliteration.

*mijito:* my grandson
*canneries:* factories where food is put into cans
*niño barrigón:* chubby little boy

# In a Neighborhood in Los Angeles

I learned
Spanish
from my grandma

*mijito*
don't cry
she'd tell me

on the mornings
my parents
would leave

to work
at the fish
canneries

my grandma
would chat
with chairs

sing them
old
songs
dance
waltzes with them
in the kitchen

when she'd say
*niño barrigón*
she'd laugh

with my grandma
I learned
to count clouds

to point out
in flowerpots
mint leaves

my grandma
wore moons
on her dress

Mexico's mountains
deserts
ocean

in her eyes
I'd see them
in her braids

I'd touch them
in her voice
smell them
one day
I was told:
she went far away

but still
I feel her
with me

whispering
in my ear
*mijito*

---

## (CA) Critical Thinking

1. What are some other examples of alliteration in this poem? **Alliteration**

2. What are some things that the speaker has learned from his grandmother? **Analyze**

3. Compare this poem to *Ramona and Her Father.* How are the family relationships similar? How are they different? **Reading/Writing Across Texts**

LOG ON ▶ Find out more about about speaker and alliteration in poetry at **www.macmillanmh.com.**

✓ **Formatting Dialogue**

Formatting dialogue helps readers easily identify the speaker in the story.

# Reading and Writing Connection

Read the passage below. Notice how author Beverly Cleary formats the dialogue to make her writing clear to the reader.

**An excerpt from**
*Ramona and Her Father*

The author uses quotation marks so the reader knows when a person is speaking. Since she uses quotation marks every time, the reader can easily figure out who is talking in the story.

Mrs. Quimby turned and faced Beezus and Ramona. "Girls, you might as well know. Your father has lost his job."

"But he liked his job," said Ramona, regretting the loss of that hamburger and those French fries eaten in the coziness of a booth. She had known her father to change jobs because he had not liked his work, but she had never heard of him losing a job.

"Was he fired?" asked Beezus, shocked at the news.

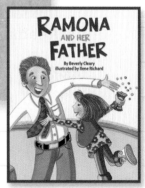

RAMONA AND HER FATHER

By Beverly Cleary
illustrated by Ilene Richard

# Read and Find

How did Roy use dialogue to show what was happening? Use the Writer's Checklist to help you.

## I Won!
### By Roy H.

"Mom, can I go over to Malik's house tomorrow after school?" My mom's face looked like she was thinking real hard about how to say "no."

How do you think this turned out?

"How are you going to catch up on all the homework if I let you go ?" She likes to answer my questions with a question.

"You mean the homework I just finished?"

## Writer's Checklist

☑ Did the author format the dialogue by using quotation marks?

☑ Does the author separate narration by using quotation marks?

☑ Are you able to easily recognize when and where a character is speaking?

# Teams at Work

**CA** **Talk About It**

In what ways do you think these team members help one another?

**LOG ON** ▶ Find out more about teams at work at www.macmillanmh.com.

111

# A ROBOT ON YOUR TEAM

## Vocabulary

| | |
|---|---|
| communicate | research |
| responsible | essential |
| specialist | decisions |

## Thesaurus

**Related Words** are words that have either similar or opposite meanings. Use a thesaurus to find words related to *specialist* to help you figure out the meaning.

Since the invention of the first machine, people keep thinking of better ways to help humans do hard jobs. Robots are a type of machine made to do work by themselves. Humans do not have to run them. Instead, people can program commands into the robot's computer. The computer program will **communicate** information to the robot.

Usually, a team of people is **responsible** for creating a robot. First, one **specialist** or more is needed to design the robot. Then other experts do **research** to find the right materials and build the robot. Finally, the team tests the robot to make sure it works correctly.

## ROBOTS AT WORK

Many workplaces use robots. For example, robots have become an **essential**, or important, part of the space program. When a team of astronauts goes into space, there are robots with them. These onboard robots have helped repair satellites and other space equipment.

Robots are smart, but they are different from humans in important ways. Robots cannot make **decisions** or think for themselves the way humans can. They "know" only what the humans program them to know.

Still, robots are able to do some amazing things, such as wrap ice cream bars and make plastic containers.

As workplaces change, teams of people will create new and better robots. Who knows how smart the next generation of robots will be?

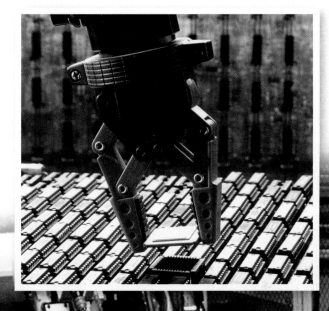

## Reread for **Comprehension**

✓ **Monitor Comprehension**

**Sequence** You can monitor your comprehension of an article by listing the article's **sequence** of events. The sequence of events is the order in which things happen. A Sequence Chart helps you understand information in an article in time order. Reread the story to find the sequence of events in creating a robot.

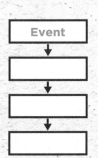

## CA Comprehension

### Genre

**Biographies** give true facts and information about real people.

### Monitor Comprehension

**Sequence**

As you read, use your Sequence Chart.

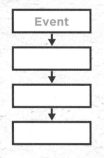

| Event |
|-------|

**Read to Find Out**
How does Ellen Ochoa become an astronaut?

# Out of this World

## The Ellen Ochoa Story

### by Liane B. Onish

"Don't be afraid to reach for the stars. I believe a good education can take you anywhere on Earth and beyond."
—Ellen Ochoa

How many people can say that their jobs are "out of this world"? Ellen Ochoa (uh-CHOH-ah) can. She is the first female Hispanic American astronaut. Her job has taken her out of this world four times.

> "One small step for man, one giant leap for mankind."
>
> —Commander Neil Armstrong

## Americans in Space

The first American astronauts were men. Alan Shepard blasted into space in 1961. Next, John Glenn became the first American to orbit, or circle, Earth in 1962. Gordon Cooper stayed in orbit for more than 24 hours in 1963. On July 20, 1969, astronaut Neil Armstrong became the first human to set foot on the moon.

But things started to change. Women astronauts would soon join the space race in a big way.

Neil Armstrong takes a photo of Buzz Aldrin while on the moon.

# Our Changing Moon

**Earth and other planets orbit the Sun. The moon orbits Earth.**

The moon orbits Earth about once every 29 days. The moon reflects light from the sun. As it orbits Earth, the moon turns and some of its reflected light cannot be seen from Earth. The moon seems to take on different shapes. These shapes are called phases.

You may have heard people talk about a quarter moon, half moon, or full moon. These are some phases of the moon. Of course, the moon does not really change its shape. It only looks that way to people on Earth.

## Phases of the Moon

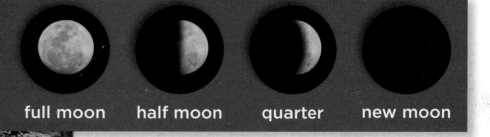

full moon   half moon   quarter   new moon

# Reaching for the Stars

Ellen Ochoa was born in California in 1958, the same year the space program began. Ochoa and other women faced a problem becoming astronauts. At first, they were not allowed to even apply for the job. Luckily, the space program began accepting women in 1978. Sally Ride, the first female astronaut, went into space in 1983. In fact, it was Sally Ride's mission that gave Ellen Ochoa the idea of becoming an astronaut.

When Ellen Ochoa began college in 1975, she thought she would be a professional musician. Then she changed her mind. When she went to Stanford University, she heard about the skills an astronaut required. She decided to try to join the astronaut program.

"I can't imagine not wanting to go into space," Ochoa says.

### Sequence
What was the first event that inspired Ellen Ochoa to become an astronaut?

**Young Ellen was a good math and science student.**

118

# Ochoa's Teamwork

At Stanford, Ochoa did **research** for several inventions. One invention of hers helps guide robotic arms for work in space. Robotic arms look like your arms with parts that move like a shoulder, an elbow, and a wrist. They do jobs that are too hard or dangerous for people.

Many tasks in outer space require astronauts to use robotic arms. Ochoa's experience with the arms helped Ochoa get into the astronaut program later in 1991.

One of Ochoa's inventions helps guide robotic arms.

# Training in Space

Ochoa had to get herself ready before she could join the space program. She began training in 1990. Her strong background in math and science helped her do well in these new classes. She also had to pass a physical exam to get into the program. And Ochoa learned to practice with the real machines astronauts use during space flights.

"In training, things keep breaking, problems have to be solved," Ochoa says. "I was in training for three years before my first mission."

During training, astronauts work on machines that get them used to working in space. One machine creates "weightlessness" conditions that astronauts feel in space.

"Weightlessness is the fun part of the mission," Ochoa says. "I guess the closest thing would be swimming or scuba diving. What is odd is that weightlessness seems more natural."

**Astronauts are trained for actual conditions in space travel.**

**Sequence**
What steps did Ellen take to become an astronaut?

# AN INTERVIEW WITH
# Ellen Ochoa

Student reporters interviewed Ellen Ochoa.
Here are some of their questions and her answers.

**What is NASA training like?**

In training, we prepare for anything that could happen on a space mission—anything that could go wrong.... Nothing has ever gone wrong on any of my missions, and our training helps us make sure that nothing will.... For my last mission, we trained for nine months before the actual flight.

**How do you sleep on the space shuttle?**

On my last mission.... we slept in what can best be described as a sleeping bag with hooks. You would find a place to hook on to, and float in.

**What do you look for in a potential astronaut, and what is their average age?**

Most of the people who are selected are between the ages of 30 to 40. We look for a college education in science or technology.... We look for people who can do many things well, because people with multiple skills can usually learn things quickly. This is a very important skill for an astronaut....

**Astronauts are able to sleep even in weightless conditions.**

# Space Work Is Teamwork

"An astronaut must be both a team player and a leader as well." Ochoa says. She tells students your age, "You should get involved in activities where you work closely with other people because working closely with other people is an **essential** part of being an astronaut!"

First, there is the ground crew. They inspect and repair the shuttle before each mission. Next, Mission Control workers guide the astronauts through each moment of a mission. They are **responsible** for knowing how equipment is working and how the astronauts are feeling.

The crew on a space shuttle must work together to get their jobs done.

Each person in Mission Control works together to make the mission a success.

During a space flight, the teamwork continues. Ochoa and the other astronauts work together to meet the goals of their mission. A space flight crew is like a sports team. The commander of the shuttle is the team captain. He or she makes the crucial **decisions** that have important effects on a mission.

On her first mission in 1993, Ellen Ochoa was a mission **specialist**. Mission specialists are scientists who do experiments. Ochoa used a robotic arm to send and get back a satellite that collected information about the sun.

Then in 1994, Ochoa was the payload commander on her second mission. The payload might be supplies or equipment, such as the robotic arm. She did satellite studies of the sun's effect on Earth's climate, or weather.

# Space Jobs

Later, Ochoa was a mission specialist again on a space flight in 1999. During this flight, she and the crew delivered supplies to the International Space Station (ISS). She also "walked" in space as she worked on the ISS.

Finally, in 2002, Ochoa took her last space flight. Again, she worked on the ISS. She used the robotic arm to deliver supplies and help build new parts of the space station.

Between missions, Ochoa worked with astronauts and ground crew to prepare for other space missions. She has worked hard planning for the International Space Station project as well.

Astronauts have to work closely together in tight spaces.

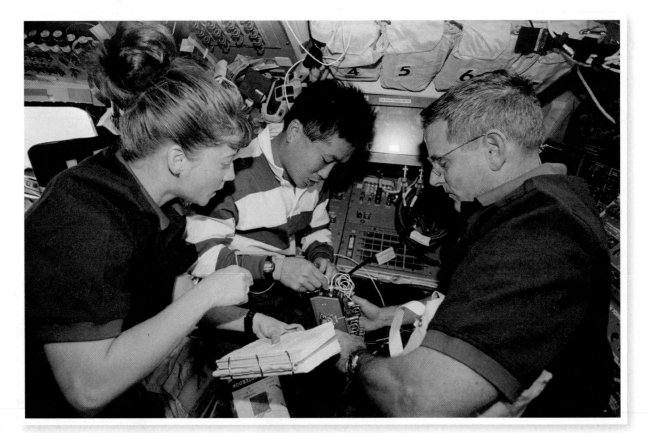

# Ellen Ochoa's Life Today

Today, Ochoa likes to travel to tell students and teachers about her experiences as an astronaut. She finds it exciting to **communicate** with students about life aboard the space shuttle.

"I'm not trying to make every kid an astronaut, but I want kids to think about a career and the preparation they'll need," Ochoa says. "I tell students that the opportunities I had were a result of having a good educational background. Education is what allows you to stand out."

Ellen Ochoa has realized her dream. She became an astronaut and she has traveled into space four times. Altogether, Ochoa has spent nearly 980 hours in space! Her space missions have taken her more than 16 million miles around Earth. That is more than 640 trips around Earth at the equator. Ellen Ochoa's job has truly taken her "out of this world!"

## BLAST OFF!

### Some facts about Ellen's trips

**STS-56 ATLAS-2 Discovery**
**Date:** April 4–17, 1993
**Time in Space:** 9 days
**Miles Traveled:** 3.9 million

**STS-66 Atlantis**
**Date:** November 3–14, 1994
**Time in Space:** 11 days
**Miles Traveled:** 4.5 million

**STS-96 Discovery**
**Date:** May 27–June 6, 1999
**Time in Space:** 10 days
**Miles Traveled:** 3.8 million

**STS-110 Atlantis**
**Date:** April 8–19, 2002
**Time in Space:** 10 days
**Miles Traveled:** 4.5 million

# Working with Liane

Liane B. Onish has been a member of many types of teams devoted to helping children learn in fun ways. She has worked as an elementary school teacher, and as a writer and editor for the Children's Television Workshop, Muppets, Disney, Warner Bros., Penguin, and Scholastic, among others. Liane now spends her time writing and editing children's books, magazines, games, and classroom materials.

Liane B. Onish

**Another book** by Liane B. Onish: *Wind and Weather*

**LOG ON** ▶ Find out more about Liane B. Onish at **www.macmillanmh.com**.

## (CA) Author's Purpose

Why did Liane B. Onish write this nonfiction article? Use details from the article to support your answer.

# CA Critical Thinking

## Summarize

Use your Sequence Chart to summarize
*Out of This World!* Retell the selection's events
in the order in which they happened.

| Event |
|-------|
| ↓ |
| |
| ↓ |
| |
| ↓ |
| |

## Think and Compare

1. In the correct **sequence**, name the steps Ellen Ochoa took to become an astronaut. **Monitor Comprehension: Sequence**

2. Reread page 119 of *Out of This World!* How does the robotic arm help make the astronauts' jobs easier? **Analyze**

3. Ellen Ochoa and her team are **responsible** for looking out for each other on a mission. What types of tasks are you responsible for? **Apply**

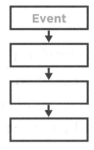

4. How might Ellen Ochoa's life be different if she had become a professional musician? How might it be the same? **Evaluate**

5. Read "A Robot on Your Team" on pages 112–113. Compare the robots described in this selection with the mechanical devices used in *Out of This World!* How are they alike? How are they different? Use details from both selections in your answer. **Reading/Writing Across Texts**

# SKY BEAR

*By Joseph Bruchac*

*Illustrated by Thomas Locker*

Long ago,
three hunters and their little dog
found the tracks of a giant bear.
They followed those tracks
all through the day
and even though it was almost dark
they did not stop, but continued on.
They saw that bear now, climbing up
a hill, which glittered
with new-fallen snow.
They ran hard to catch it,
but the bear was too fast.
They ran and they ran, climbing
up and up until one of the
hunters said,
"Brothers, look down."
They did and saw they
were high above Earth.

What image do you see when you read "they were high above Earth"?

Sky Bear "running on through the stars" gives readers an image of what Sky Bear really is.

That bear was Sky Bear,
running on through the stars.
Look up now
and you will see her,
circling the sky.

## CA Critical Thinking

1. What imagery in the poem helps you see the image of the bear in the sky? **Imagery**

2. How is this narrative poem like a story? Find the beginning, middle, and end. **Analyze**

3. Compare the hunters' interest in Sky Bear with Ellen Ochoa and the astronauts' interests in *Out of This World!* How are their experiences similar? **Reading/Writing Across Text**

 **LOG ON** ▶ Find out more about poetry at **www.macmillanmh.com**.

## Writing

### Formatting Dialogue

Quotation marks will help the reader identify which character in the story is speaking.

# Reading and Writing Connection

Read the passage below. Notice how author Liane Onish formats the dialogue to make clear who is speaking.

**An excerpt from**
***Out of this World! The Ellen Ochoa Story***

The author uses quotation marks so the reader knows when a person is talking. Quotation marks are a signal to the reader to imagine someone speaking.

During training, astronauts work on machines that get them used to working in space. One machine creates weightlessness conditions that astronauts feel in space.

"Weightlessness is the fun part of the mission," Ochoa says. "I guess the closest thing would be swimming or scuba diving. What is odd is that weightlessness seems more natural."

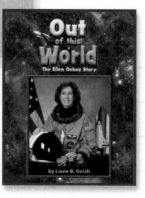

# Read and Find

Read Lola's situation below. How did she use dialogue to show what was happening? Use the Writer's Checklist to help you.

## Pass the Ketchup
### By Lola J.

"Please pass the ketchup?" I asked my brother.

"What are you going to do for me?" He asked with a goofy grin.

"Umm ... nothing!" I replied with my best goofy grin.

"Guys, that's enough." My father had had enough.

Read how my father handles this.

# Writer's Checklist

✓ Did the author use quotation marks at the beginning and the end of each piece of dialogue?

✓ Does the author separate narration from dialogue using quotation marks?

☑ Are you able to easily recognize when and where a character is speaking?

# World Cup Worries

Fabio was all set to watch the World Cup match. His favorite team was playing—Brazil. Just as he sat down, Fabio's father called, "Fabio, come here, please."

"But Dad, the World Cup is starting!" cried Fabio.

"That may be," said Mr. Silva. "But that doesn't change the fact that you have chores to do."

Work during the big match? Fabio really wanted to ignore his father and watch the game. He decided that if he did his chores really fast, he could still catch most of the match.

"What do you need me to do, Dad?" asked Fabio.

"You can start by cleaning your room," Mr. Silva said.

"Okay," said Fabio. He was relieved because he knew he could get that job done fast. He threw clothes in the hamper, put books on the bookshelf, and straightened up his shoes. In 20 minutes, his room looked tidy—sort of.

"I'm done, Dad!" yelled Fabio. He hurried into the other room to turn on the television.

"Great," said Mr. Silva. "Now you can help me with the yard work."

Fabio sighed. He knew that yard work could take the rest of the day. "Dad, that means we'll miss the whole match!"

"This is more important," said Mr. Silva. He gave Fabio some gardening gloves and some trash bags, and put him to work cleaning up.

"Dad, I thought you loved watching the World Cup," said Fabio.

"I do," said Mr. Silva, "but work should be done while the sun shines."

After a few hours of hard work, Mr. Silva said that it was time for a break. Fabio was gloomy since he'd missed the whole match. He barely said a word as his father fixed him a snack.

"Fabio, I know you wanted to watch the match," said Mr. Silva. "I appreciate that you made the choice to help me, instead."

"I'm not sure I had a choice, Dad," replied Fabio.

"You can always choose to do the wrong thing," explained his father, "but you didn't. Now, here's the good news. I taped the game while we worked. Let's watch it while we eat!"

"All right! That sounds like a great choice, Dad," laughed Fabio.

# Susan B. Anthony

## *A Pioneer for Women's Rights*

**SUSAN B. ANTHONY** was born to a Quaker family. Quakers believe in justice and fair treatment for everyone. In the early 1800s, most girls were not given an education equal to that of boys, but the Quakers allowed both boys and girls to have equal educations. In religious meetings both Quaker girls and boys could speak out. And women could vote on church matters.

After Susan B. Anthony met Elizabeth Cady Stanton, they became close friends and leaders in the women's suffrage movement. The suffrage movement worked to get women the right to vote. Anthony and Stanton were a great team. Their goal was to change the United States Constitution and give women the right to vote.

## Women Can Vote!

*This time line shows important dates in Susan B. Anthony's life and in the women's suffrage movement.*

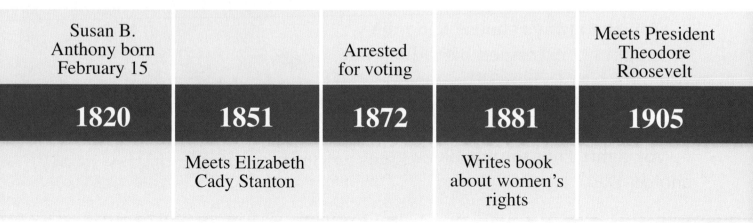

| Susan B. Anthony born February 15 | | Arrested for voting | | Meets President Theodore Roosevelt |
|---|---|---|---|---|
| **1820** | **1851** | **1872** | **1881** | **1905** |
| | Meets Elizabeth Cady Stanton | | Writes book about women's rights | |

In 1872, Anthony brought 15 women to vote in a national election. She was arrested. At her trial the judge said that Anthony did not have the right to vote. Anthony refused to pay the $100 fine.

Anthony continued to work for women's suffrage throughout her life. She made many trips across the country and gave lectures about why women's rights were important. During her life Anthony published several newspapers. With Elizabeth Stanton and Matilda Gage, she wrote a book about the suffrage movement.

Susan B. Anthony died in 1906. In 1920 the Nineteenth Amendment was finally passed. This amendment gave women the right to vote. Because of all of Anthony's hard work, this law is sometimes called the Susan B. Anthony Amendment.

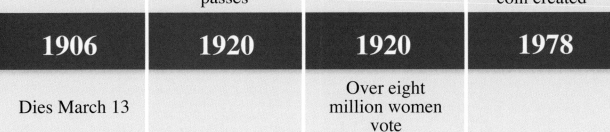

|  | 19th Amendment passes |  | Susan B. Anthony dollar coin created |  |
| --- | --- | --- | --- | --- |
| **1906** | **1920** | **1920** | **1978** |  |
| Dies March 13 |  | Over eight million women vote |  |  |

# CA Critical Thinking

**Now answer Numbers 1 through 4. Base your answers on the passage "World Cup Worries."**

1. **How does Fabio's dad solve Fabio's problem in this passage?**

   A  Fabio's dad allows him to take a break and watch the game.

   B  Fabio's dad decides they can do the work the next day.

   C  Fabio's dad brings Fabio to the soccer game.

   D  Fabio's dad tapes the soccer game.

2. **Which word from the story can mean both "to take a rest from work" AND "to damage"?**

   A  match

   B  straightened

   C  break

   D  trash

3. **Which word BEST describes Fabio's dad in this passage?**

   A  fair

   B  tricky

   C  foolish

   D  unkind

4. **Describe the events that happen on the day described in the passage. What happens first, second, and last? Use details from the passage to support your answer.**

**Now answer Numbers 1 through 4. Base your answers on the passage "Susan B. Anthony: A Pioneer for Women's Rights."**

**1.** **Look at the time line. Which of the following events happened FIRST?**

    **A**   Susan B. Anthony meets President Roosevelt.
    **B**   Susan B. Anthony is arrested.
    **C**   Susan B. Anthony meets Elizabeth Cady Stanton.
    **D**   A Susan B. Anthony dollar coin is created.

**2.** **What conclusion can you draw about Susan B. Anthony?**

    **A**   She was hardworking.
    **B**   Her friends were irresponsible.
    **C**   As she grew older, she grew lazy.
    **D**   She never lived in Washington, D.C.

**3.** **Look at the time line. Which of the following events happened LAST?**

    **A**   women get the right to vote
    **B**   Susan B. Anthony Amendment passes
    **C**   Susan B. Anthony is arrested
    **D**   the Susan B. Anthony dollar coin is created

**4.** **What conclusion can you draw from this passage?**

    **A**   Women had fewer rights than they do today.
    **B**   Girls were not allowed in Quaker schools.
    **C**   Only half of the women in the country voted.
    **D**   Only women attended Susan B. Anthony's lectures.

## Write on Demand

**PROMPT** Name one other important woman in history and tell why she is important. Use details from the article to support your answer. Write for 10 minutes. Write as much as you can, as well as you can.

# The Big Question

**What makes each animal unique?**

**Theme Launcher Video**

 **LOG ON** Find out more about unique animals at **www.macmillanmh.com**.

## The Big Question

**What makes each animal unique?**

Every animal has special qualities that helps it to survive. Some animals, such as penguins, have unique bodies to protect them in their environment. Other animals, such as the duck-billed platypus, have unique body parts that enable them to get food commonly found in their environment.

Over long periods of time, animals can adapt. Adaptations are when an animal changes its body shape or color, adjusts its methods of getting and eating food, or changes how it defends itself or cares for its young.

## Research Activities

Throughout the unit, you will read about unique animals. Think of an animal with a unique quality or adaptation that you would like to learn more about. Do research to find out what makes this animal special. Write a report about this unique animal.

## Keep Track of Ideas

As you read, keep track of the unique animals that you are learning about. Use the Accordion Book to organize your information. On each fold, write what you learn each week about different unique animals.

**FOLDABLES®**
**Study Organizer**

Unit Theme | Week 1 | Week 2 | Week 3 | Week 4 | Week 5

# Research Toolkit

## Conduct Your Unit 5 Research Online with:

### Research Roadmap
Follow step-by-step guide to complete your research project.

### Online Resources
- Topic Finder and other Research Tools
- Videos and Virtual Fieldtrips
- Photos and Drawings for Presentations
- Related Articles and Web Resources

### California Web Site Links

**LOG ON** ▷ Go to **www.macmillanmh.com** for more information.

## California People

**Harry Wegeforth**
**Doctor**
Doctor Wegeforth founded a hospital, but he was best known for being the founder of the San Diego Zoo.

# Antarctic Life

**CA** **Talk About It**

Antarctica is a cold, icy place. What is unique about the animals that live there?

**LOG ON** Find out more about Antarctic life at **www.macmillanmh.com**.

# Life in Antarctica

*by Kenji Foster*

The coldest and iciest place on Earth is Antarctica. There, the temperature hardly ever gets above freezing, even in the summer. Believe it or not, some things can live in such a frozen land.

## Plants

In the coldest months, a **fierce** wind whips the air across Antarctica. Those strong, blowing winds make the air so chilly that there is little rain. Simple plants without leaves, such as mosses and lichens (LIGH•kuhnz), are the only kinds that can live in Antarctica. These plants grow on rocks near the coast, where it is a little warmer.

## Seabirds

Penguins, Antarctic terns, and brown skuas are three kinds of birds that live in Antarctica. If you listen closely, you may hear a penguin's bark as it **echoes**—bouncing off the icy land and softly repeating. Each penguin **shuffles** along the ice. Then they get together in a **huddle**, or tight group, to keep warm. New chicks have a layer of soft, fluffy feathers called **down**. As they grow into **junior** penguins, they begin to develop stiff, waterproof feathers. Now they can swim in cold water. While penguins live in Antarctica all year, the terns and the brown skuas only visit in the summer.

## Seals and Whales

Blue whales, humpback whales, and southern right whales spend their summers in Antarctica as well. They have plenty of fat to keep them warm. Leopard seals, as well as Ross, Weddell, and crabeater seals, rely on thick fur for warmth. Crabeater seals travel well on land, but leopard, Ross, and Weddell seals move fastest when they stay **down** below the surface of the icy water.

## Reread for **Comprehension**

### Summarize

**Main Idea and Details** A **main idea** is the most important point that an author makes about a topic. **Details** tell about the main idea. A main idea can be stated or not stated. Use details to figure out an unstated main idea.

A Main Idea Chart can help you summarize a paragraph or section of text. Reread the selection to find the main idea and the supporting details that tell about it.

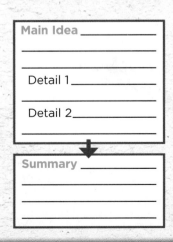

Main Idea _____
_____

Detail 1 _____

Detail 2 _____

Summary _____
_____
_____

**Comprehension**

## Genre

**Nonfiction** Narrative nonfiction is a story, or account, about actual living things.

## Summarize

**Main Idea and Details**
As you read, use your Main Idea Chart.

| Main Idea _____ |
| --- |
| _____ |
| _____ |
| Detail 1_____ |
| _____ |
| Detail 2_____ |
| _____ |

| Summary _____ |
| --- |
| _____ |
| _____ |
| _____ |

## Read to Find Out

How does the father penguin take care of the penguin chick?

# Penguin Chick

By Betty Tatham
Illustrated by Helen K. Davie

Award
Winning
Selection

A **fierce** wind howls. It whips snow across the ice.
Here, a female emperor penguin has just laid an egg.
It is the only egg she will lay this year.

147

Most birds build nests for their eggs. But on the ice in Antarctica, there are no twigs or leaves. There is no grass or mud. Nothing to build a nest with. Nothing but snow and ice.

The new penguin father uses his beak to scoop the egg onto his webbed feet.

He tucks it under his feather-covered skin, into a special place called a brood patch. The egg will be as snug and warm there as if it were in a sleeping bag.

One of the penguin parents must stay with the egg to keep it warm. But where penguins lay their eggs, there is no food for them to eat.

The penguin father is bigger and fatter than the mother. He can live longer without food. So the father penguin stays with the egg while the mother travels to the sea to find food.

The two parents sing together before the mother penguin leaves.

Along with many other penguins, the mother penguin leaves the rookery, where she laid her egg.

The mother walks or slides on her belly. This is called tobogganing. She uses her flippers and webbed feet to push herself forward over ice and snow.

**Main Idea and Details**
What is the main idea of the first paragraph?

Because it's winter in Antarctica, water near the shore is frozen for many miles. After three days the mother penguin comes to the end of the ice.

FISH

SQUID

KRILL

She dives into the water to hunt for fish, squid, and tiny shrimplike creatures called krill.

Back at the rookery, the penguin fathers form a group called a **huddle**. They stand close together for warmth. Each one keeps his own egg warm.

**Main Idea and Details**
What is the main idea of this paragraph?

For two months the penguin father always keeps his egg on his feet. When he walks, he **shuffles** his feet so the egg doesn't roll away. He sleeps standing up. He has no food to eat, but the fat on his body keeps him alive.

Finally he feels the chick move inside the egg. The chick pecks and pecks and pecks. In about three days the egg cracks open.

The chick is wet. But soon his soft feathers, called **down**, dry and become fluffy and gray. The father still keeps the chick warm in the brood patch. Sometimes the chick pokes his head out. But while he's so little, he must stay covered. And he must stay on his father's feet. Otherwise the cold would kill him.

The father talks to the chick in his trumpet voice. The chick answers with a whistle.

The father's trumpet call **echoes** across the ice. The penguin mother is on her way back to the rookery, but she can't hear him. She's still too far away. If the mother doesn't come back soon with food, the chick will die.

Two days pass before the mother can hear the father penguin's call.

At last the mother arrives at the rookery. She cuddles close to her chick and trumpets to him. He whistles back. With her beak she brushes his soft gray down.

The mother swallowed many fish before she left the ocean. She brings some of this food back up from her stomach and feeds her chick. She has enough food to keep him fed for weeks. He stays on her feet and snuggles into her brood patch.

The father is very hungry, so he travels to open water. There he dives to hunt for food. Weeks later the father returns with more food for the chick.

Each day the parents preen, or brush, the chick's downy coat with their beaks. This keeps the down fluffy and keeps the chick warm.

As the chick gets bigger, he and the other chicks no longer need to stay on their parents' feet. Instead they stay together to keep warm.

This group of chicks is called a crèche, or a nursery. The chick now spends most of his time here. But he still rushes to his mother or father to be fed when either one comes back from the ocean.

Sometimes the chick and the other young penguins dig their beaks into the ice to help them walk up a slippery hill. They toboggan **down** fast on their fluffy bellies.

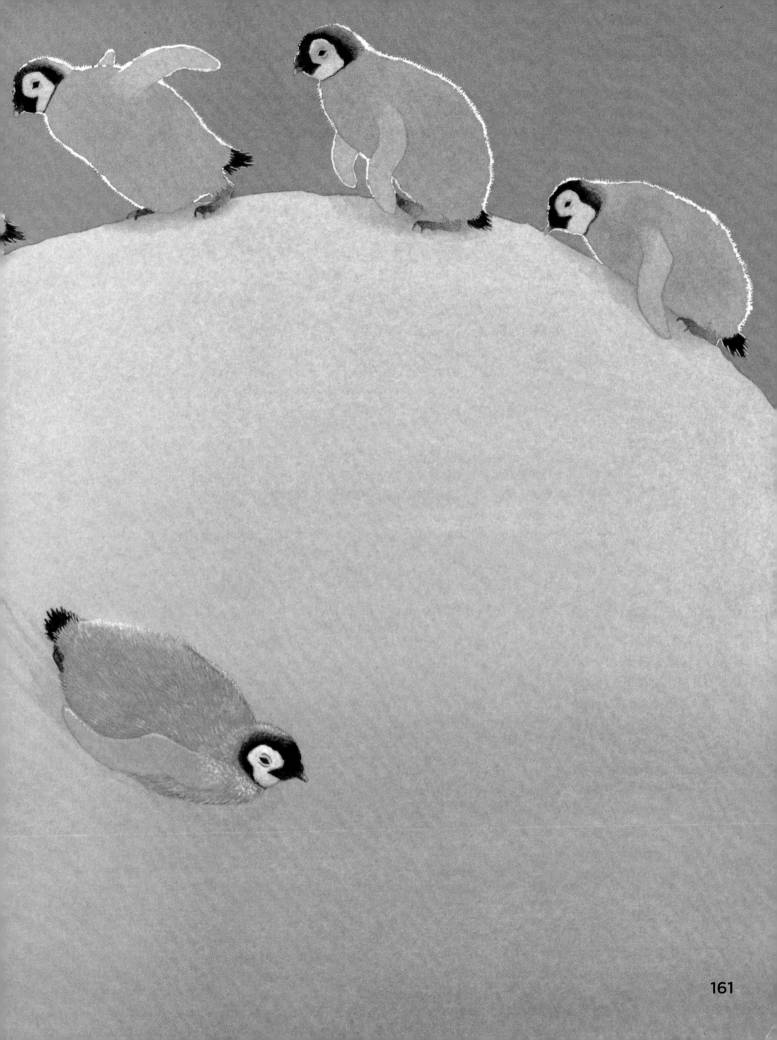

The chick grows and grows. After five months, he has grown into a **junior** penguin. He is old enough to travel to the ocean.

| WINTER | | SPRING | |
|---|---|---|---|
| August | September | October |

Now he has a waterproof coat of feathers, instead of fluffy down. He can swim in the icy cold ocean because his feathers keep him dry and warm.

| November | December | SUMMER January |
| --- | --- | --- |

164

The young penguin spends most of his time in the water. He swims, flapping his flippers as if he were flying underwater. He uses his webbed feet to steer wherever he wants to go.

He catches a fish with his beak and swallows it headfirst.

Now the young penguin can catch his own food and take care of himself. In about five years he'll find a mate. Then he'll take care of his own egg until the chick can hatch.

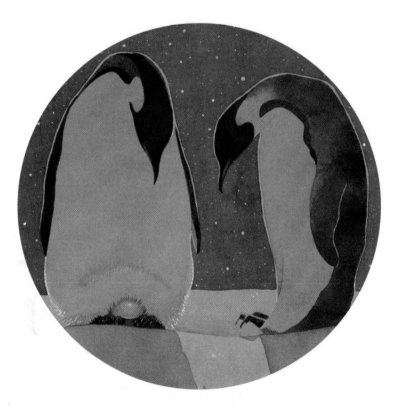

# Chill Out with Betty and Helen!

## Author

**Betty Tatham** likes writing nonfiction books about animals for children. She became interested in writing after years of teaching children to enjoy nature and write their own stories. Betty works hard at being an author. She has taken writing classes and attended special conferences for writers.

**Other books** by Betty Tatham: *How Animals Communicate* and *How Animals Play*

## Illustrator

**Helen K. Davie** has chilly memories of her work on this story. She went to Sea World in San Diego and spent time in the emperor penguins' frozen habitat. Helen got an up-close look at the birds so she could draw them better.

## CA Author's Purpose

Nonfiction authors often write to explain or persuade. Why did Betty Tatham write *Penguin Chick*? What clues help you figure out her purpose?

 **LOG ON** Find out more about Betty Tatham and Helen K. Davie at **www.macmillanmh.com**.

# CA Critical Thinking

## Summarize

Use your Main Idea Chart to help you summarize *Penguin Chick.* Include the most important ideas and supporting details about the life of an emperor penguin chick.

| Main Idea _____ |
| _____ |
| _____ |
| Detail 1_____ |
| Detail 2_____ |
| _____ |

| Summary _____ |
| _____ |
| _____ |
| _____ |

## Think and Compare

1. Describe the **fierce** conditions in Antarctica. Tell the **main idea** and **details** that explain why it is hard for penguin chicks to survive there. **Summarize: Main Idea and Details**

2. Tell about a penguin chick's life from the time it hatches until it can take care of itself. Use details in your answer. **Synthesize**

3. Emperor penguins work as a team. Discuss the ways you work as a member of a team. **Apply**

4. In what ways are emperor penguins like other animals and their young? **Evaluate**

5. What is the common main idea in "Life in Antarctica" and *Penguin Chick*? Use details from both selections to support your answer. **Reading/Writing Across Texts**

# Antarctic Anthem

(CA) **Poetry**

**Poetry** uses elements such as rhyme, rhythm, and repetition to express feelings and ideas.

## ✔ Literary Elements

**Rhythmic Patterns** are series of stressed and unstressed syllables.

**Imagery** is the use of words to create a picture in the reader's mind.

At the bottom of the planet
Lies a land of ice and granite:
*Ant · arc · ti · ca! Ant · arc · ti · ca!*
Where winter days are dark-tica.
It's the continent of our birth;
It's the coldest place on Earth:
*Ant · arc · ti · ca! Ant · arc · ti · ca!*
You'd better wear your park-tica,
Or the brutal, blasting blizzards
Will freeze your beaks and gizzards.
*Ant · arc · ti · ca! Ant · arc · ti · ca!*

Breaking "Antarctica" into syllables and repeating it again and again creates a rhythmic pattern in the poem.

Come visit on a lark-tica!
We'll snuggle in the snow
When it's thirty-five below.
*Ant · arc · ti · ca! Ant · arc · ti · ca!*
It's grander than New York-tica.
Skyscraping icebergs roam
All across the frosty foam
In our sweet Antarctic home.

— *Judy Sierra*

This line uses imagery to paint a picture of icebergs being as big as skyscrapers.

## CA Connect and Compare

1. Which words in this poem help the reader visualize an image of Antarctica? **Imagery**

2. An anthem is the official song of a country or place. How are the words of "Antarctic Anthem" like a song? **Evaluate**

3. Compare "Antarctic Anthem" with *Penguin Chick.* Which selection gives you more information about life in Antarctica? Explain. **Reading/Writing Across Texts**

LOG ON ▶ Find out more at **www.macmillanmh.com**.

# Writing

## ✔ Chronological Order

Good writers use chronological order to tell the events in the order in which they happen.

# Reading and Writing Connection

Read the passage below. Notice how author Betty Tatham shows us the order in which things happen after the chick is born.

**An excerpt from**
*Penguin Chick*

The author tells us what happens after the feathers dry and what the father and chick do next to keep warm.

The chick is wet. But soon his soft feathers, called down, dry and become fluffy and gray. The father still keeps the chick warm in the brood patch. Sometimes the chick pokes his head out. But while he's so little, he must stay covered. And he must stay on his father's feet. Otherwise the cold would kill him.

Penguin Chick
By Betty Tatham
Illustrated by Helen K. Davie

# Read and Find

Read Alexandra's writing below. How did she order
the events to show exactly what was happening?
Use the Writer's Checklist to help you.

# Bowling

### By Alexandra P.

I picked up a pink ball and staggered
from the weight. I held the ball and
focused on the arrows in front of
me to try to make my ball go straight
down the middle of the alley. I swung
the ball between my legs and let the
ball go. The ball began to knock down
the pins. Yes! I had a strike!

Read about
my bowling
experience.

# Writer's Checklist

 Did the author describe her actions in an order
that makes sense to you?

 Does the author show a beginning, a middle, and
an end?

☐ Does it feel as if you are watching what happened?

## Talk About It

What does this animal home have in common with people's homes?

LOG ON ▶ Find out more about animal homes at **www.macmillanmh.com**.

# ANiMAL HOMES

## Vocabulary

| | |
|---|---|
| architects | retreats |
| structures | shallow |
| contain | shelter |

## Context Clues

**Homophones** are words that sound the same but have different spellings and meanings. If you are not sure which word is used, look at the surrounding words or phrases to figure out the meaning.

# Web Spinners

*by Steven Kutner*

Just as bees build hives to live in, spiders spin webs. Spiders are talented **architects**. They design and build **structures** to live in that are works of art. These structures are also traps for other insects.

### Spinning Silk

Spider webs are made from silk. Spiders make silk in their bellies. Their silk-making gland has many tiny holes. First, the silk goes through the holes to get outside the spider's body. Next, the silk meets the air, and forms a thread. The thread is very thin but very strong.

Spiders can make different kinds of silk. Some **contain** a material that makes the silk sticky. Other silks do not have this material.

Finally, a spider can spin a thread behind itself everywhere it goes. This thread is called a dragline. If an enemy comes near, the spider **retreats** on its dragline. Being able to go backward on its own line is like having a self-made escape route!

## Tangled Webs

Different spiders build different kinds of webs. The simplest web is called a tangled web. It is just a mess of threads that are attached to something. A cobweb is a dusty, old, tangled web.

## Cellar Spiders

Some spiders are called cellar spiders. This is because they usually build tangled webs in cellars or other dark places.

## Orb Weavers

The most common webs are shaped like wheels. They are built by orb weavers. You can find these webs in open areas, such as the spaces between branches.

## Water Spiders

The water spider builds its web in tiny ponds and other places with **shallow** water. The web looks like a small air-filled balloon. The water spider feeds and raises its family inside this cozy **shelter**.

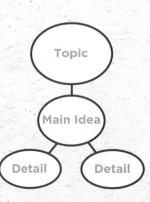

## Reread for **Comprehension**

### Summarize

**Description** Authors sometimes organize information by using **description**. Signal words such as *first, next, finally,* or *for example* tell readers that descriptive facts are coming up in the text.

Reread the selection. Use your Description Web to record the details about one topic.

Topic

Main Idea

Detail     Detail

# Comprehension

### Genre

**Nonfiction** Informational nonfiction is a detailed explanation of real things using facts.

### Summarize

**Description** As you read, use your Description Web.

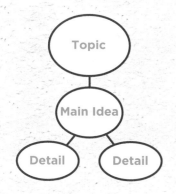

### Read to Find Out

How are some animal homes similar to your home?

# Animal Homes

by Ann O. Squire

# Why Do Animals Need Homes?

Animals need homes for many of the same reasons that people do. What are some of those reasons? Start by thinking about your own home, and the kinds of things you do there.

Some kinds of penguins build nests to protect their chicks.

Eating is one very important thing you do every day. Your house has a kitchen where you store and prepare food. Some animals also keep food in their homes. Honeybees, for example, live in hives made up of waxy honeycombs. Each honeycomb has many six-sided cubbies, or cells, where the bees store their honey.

The cells of the honeycomb are also used as nurseries for young bees. And that may remind you of another reason people and animals need homes. They need a safe place to raise their young. Birds' nests, alligator mounds, and the dens of polar bears are other kinds of homes made for raising a family.

> **Description**
> What are two ways honeybees use their hives?

▲ Other cells are used as nurseries for bee larvae.

Bees store honey in some ▶ of the cells of their hive.

A desert tortoise in its burrow

Doesn't it feel good to come indoors on a cold winter day or turn up the air conditioner on a hot and humid summer night? That's another reason we need a home—to protect us from bad weather.

The desert tortoise lives in dry parts of the southwestern United States, where summer temperatures often go above 100 degrees Fahrenheit (38 degrees Celsius). To escape the heat, the tortoise digs a **shallow** burrow, or hole, where it can rest during the hottest part of the day.

In the winter, when temperatures fall below freezing, the tortoise digs a much deeper burrow. Then it climbs in and spends the winter there, hibernating with other tortoises.

Underground burrows also give animals a place to hide from their enemies. Prairie dogs, for example, dig long, winding burrows with many different rooms and tunnels.

Many people's homes have a front door, a back door, and maybe even a side door. A prairie-dog burrow has several openings, too. If a hungry predator invades the burrow through the main entrance, the prairie dogs can escape out the back way.

> **Description**
> Use facts and details to describe a prairie-dog burrow.

A prairie dog standing near its burrow entrance

**A coyote trying to invade a prairie-dog burrow**

Some animals build homes for more tricky reasons. Many spiders spin webs mainly to trap unlucky insects.

Now that you know some of the reasons animals need homes, let's find out about some unusual animal homes.

A weaverbird building its nest

# Building a Home

Many animals build their own homes. These animal **architects** can be birds, mammals, insects, and even fish.

The African weaverbird's name is a clue to the way this bird builds its nest. The male weaverbird gathers long blades of grass, which he knots and weaves into a sturdy ring. Then he adds grass to the ring, making a hollow ball. To keep out tree snakes, the ball is open only at the bottom. When the nest is finished, the weaverbird calls to attract nearby females. If a female likes the nest, she moves in, and the two raise a family.

◀ A spider trapping prey in its web

Termite towers have many rooms.

Some insects build homes, too. One of the largest and most complicated **structures** in the animal world is created by tiny African termites.

A termite tower may be as tall as a giraffe and **contain** millions of termites. The walls of the tower are made of a rock-hard mixture of dirt and saliva. They contain air shafts that keep the inside of the tower cool, even in the blazing sun.

The tower has many special rooms. It has a royal chamber, where the termite king and queen live, nurseries for the young, rooms for storing food, and even an underground garden. Most termites live for only a few years, but a termite tower may last for close to a century.

A termite tower in Ghana, Africa

Beavers use sticks and mud to build a dam. Then they build their lodge in the middle of the pond formed by the dam.

Have you ever heard people say someone is as "busy as a beaver"? You'd know what they mean if you saw how much work goes into building a beaver lodge.

First, the beavers use sticks and mud to make a dam across a stream. Then water backs up behind the dam to form a pond. In the center of the pond, the beavers build their lodge. It looks like nothing more than a pile of sticks, but the lodge has a room inside that is reached by underwater tunnels. The beavers can come and go easily, but it's almost impossible for wolves and other predators to find a way in.

**The hermit crab makes its home in an empty seashell.**

# Finding a Home

Bees, weaverbirds, termites, and beavers all work long and hard to build their homes. But some animals take the easy way out. They look around for ready-made lodgings.

Unlike most other crabs, the hermit crab does not have a hard shell to protect it. It needs a safe place to live, so the hermit crab searches for an empty snail shell. When it finds a shell that fits, the hermit crab squeezes inside. It stays there until it grows too big for that shell. Then it must look for a larger shell.

The pea crab doesn't even wait until a shell is empty. This tiny crab moves in with the original owner! It squeezes into the shell of a mussel, clam, or oyster while that animal is still alive. The shellfish isn't even bothered by the pea crab sharing its home. As the shellfish filters food through its gills, the pea crab catches tiny bits of food as they float past.

**A pea crab**

A white cowbird egg in a nest containing blue wood thrush eggs

A cowbird chick being raised by a yellow warbler

The cowbird is even more daring. Instead of building its own nest, the female cowbird searches the forest for other nesting birds. When she sees a likely couple, she settles down to wait.

As soon as the unsuspecting birds leave their nest, the cowbird darts in and throws out one of their eggs. Then she quickly lays one of her own. The nesting birds never know the difference! They raise the cowbird chick as if it were one of their own.

Burrowing owls ▶

Birds don't usually live underground, but one that does is the burrowing owl. These long-legged owls sometimes move into abandoned prairie-dog burrows. The birds come out in the cool of the evening to hunt small rodents, frogs, and insects.

# Mobile Homes

**A turtle can protect itself by retreating into its shell.**

Most people and most animals live in homes that stay in one place. But if you've ever traveled in a camper, trailer, or boat, you know that some kinds of homes can move around with you. Did you know that some animals also live in "mobile homes"?

Tortoises and turtles move slowly. You might think they would be easy prey for any animal that wanted to eat them. But tortoises and turtles can escape into the safety of their homes in a flash, simply by pulling their head and feet inside their hard shell.

**Turtles sunning themselves on a log**

The snail is another animal that carries its house on its back. Snails need damp conditions in order to survive. In cold or dry weather, the snail **retreats** into its spiral shell to avoid drying out.

Like turtles, snails can retreat into their shells.

A kind of caterpillar called the bagworm makes its home out of twigs woven together with silk. The bagworm lives inside this silken case and drags its **shelter** along as it moves from branch to branch feeding on leaves.

**A bagworm hanging from a spruce tree**

191

## AUTHOR
## Ann O. Squire

is an expert on how animals behave. Before Ann began to write books for children, she studied many different kinds of animals. She has studied everything from rats to the African electric fish.

**Other books** by Ann O. Squire: *Growing Crystals* and *Seashells*

**LOG ON** Find out more about Ann O. Squire at www.macmillanmh.com.

## CA Author's Purpose

Nonfiction authors often write to inform or persuade. Why did Ann O. Squire write *Animal Homes*? What are some clues that help you figure out her purpose?

# 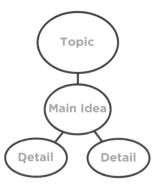 Critical Thinking

## Summarize

Use the Description Web to help you summarize facts about *Animal Homes*. Create a topic sentence about animal homes. Then describe the main ideas using details about different animal homes.

Topic

Main Idea

Detail    Detail

## Think and Compare

1. Choose an animal that carries its **shelter** around. Using details from the text and your Description Web, **describe** that animal and its home. **Summarize: Description**

2. Reread pages 190–191 of *Animal Homes*. Describe mobile homes and the animals that live in them. How is a mobile home more useful than a nest or web? Use details from the selection in your answer. **Analyze**

3. Which animal home in this selection would you like to learn more about? Explain your answer. **Synthesize**

4. Why is studying animal homes important for people? **Evaluate**

5. Read "Web Spinners" on pages 174–175. Look at the photographs in the two selections you have read. Compare the structures of the spider webs with the structure of another animal home. Use details from both selections in your answer.
**Reading/Writing Across Texts**

(CA) **Science**

**Genre**

Nonfiction gives information about real people, places, or things.

✔ **Text Feature**

Directions help you follow the steps in a process.

**Content Vocabulary**

personality

behavior

individual

# Do Animals Have Personalities?

*by Patricia West*

Everyone has a **personality**, or a unique way of acting and thinking. One person might love to run and jump. Another might prefer to sit and think. Your next-door neighbor could be very shy, but your cousin might be friendly to everyone. Each of these people has a different personality.

Animals also have personalities. Scientists study their **behavior**, or the way they act, in order to learn more about them. Here are three **individual** animals that have special personalities.

## What a Bell Can Tell

A cat named Phoenix doesn't need anyone to open doors for him. When he wants to go out, he just pushes a special doorbell.

The doorbell's inventor thought that many people would rush to buy cat doorbells, but few have been sold. That might be because not many cats have the same independent personality as Phoenix.

### Following Directions

Here's an experiment to find out something interesting about a cat. It will tell you whether a cat is "right-pawed" or "left-pawed."

## Is Your Cat Right-Pawed or Left-Pawed?

### What to Do

1. Use the spoon to put a little cat food in the bottle.

2. Put the bottle on its side near the cat.

3. When the cat uses its paw to get the food, write down whether the cat uses its right or left paw.

4. Repeat Steps 1–3 several times.

5. Count the number of times the cat uses its right paw and the number of times it uses its left paw.

6. Decide whether your cat is right-pawed, left-pawed, or both.

### What You Need

- a hungry cat
- a small, empty plastic bottle with a narrow opening just big enough for the cat's paw
- a little food that the cat likes
- a spoon

## Pumpkin Play

Scientists at Seattle's Woodland Park Zoo gave carved pumpkins to their gorillas. They observed how their gorillas played with the pumpkins before eating them.

A gorilla called Zuri grabbed as many pumpkins as he could. Another gorilla, Jumoke, spent a lot of time picking out the biggest pumpkin. Alafia looked for a pumpkin she could fit over her head. Congo chose a pumpkin with a face he liked best. Each gorilla showed his or her personality while making choices.

## Brilliant Birdbrain

Most parrots can only repeat words their owners say, but one parrot, named Alex, is a talker *and* a good listener! When his owner holds up a tray with different objects, Alex can pick out the yellow object, the biggest object, or even "the one under the square."

Alex also has a good memory. If his owner asks, "Alex, what color is corn?" Alex answers, "Yellow." He can do this even if there is no corn in sight to give him a hint.

 **Critical Thinking**

1. Look at the experiment on page 195. Explain the directions in Step 4. **Following Directions**

2. Why do you think people like pets with interesting personalities? Explain. **Analyze**

3. Compare the cowbird in *Animal Homes* with the parrot in this selection. What does each bird's behavior tell you about its personality? Use details from both selections in your answer. **Reading/Writing Across Texts**

 **Science Activity**

Research an animal with unusual abilities. Write a paragraph that tells about three new things you learned in your research.

 Find out more about unusual animals at **www.macmillanmh.com**.

## Writing

**CA**

### ✔ Chronological Order

Putting events in chronological order helps create a clear picture in the reader's mind.

Read the passage below. Notice how author Ann Squire puts the events in an order. This gives you a clear picture of what is happening.

**An excerpt from**
*Animal Homes*

The author writes about how the bird builds its nest in the order in which it happens.

The African weaverbird's name is a clue to the way this bird builds its nest. The male weaverbird gathers long blades of grass, which he knots and weaves into a sturdy ring. Then he adds grass to the ring, making a hollow ball. To keep out tree snakes, the ball is open only at the bottom. When the nest is finished, the weaverbird calls to attract nearby females. If a female likes the nest, she moves in, and the two raise a family.

# Read and Find

Read Kelsie's writing below. Did she write in an order that clearly shows what was happening? Use the Writer's Checklist to help you.

# Clubhouse
## By Kelsie W.

My friend and I built a private place. We called it our clubhouse. We took rope, blankets, sheets, and pillows and we found a place in the back yard. We tied the rope to one tree and pulled it to another tree and tied the end there. We draped the blankets over the rope and put the sheets on the ground.

Read about how I built my clubhouse.

# Writer's Checklist

 Did the author show us the steps she took to build the clubhouse in a logical order?

 Does the author show a beginning, a middle, and an end?

 Does it feel as if you are watching what happened?

199

# Talk About It

What do animals need to survive? Why is it important that we share the planet with animals?

 **LOG ON** ▶ Find out more about animals on the move at **www.macmillanmh.com**.

TIME
FOR KIDS®

# Animals on the Move

# Daddy Daycare

**Dad to the rescue! A father protects his baby from a baboon bully.**

Scientists have discovered that baboon moms aren't on the job alone. Studies show that baboon dads help care for their young, too. Male baboons can identify their kids by the way the young ones look and smell.

With their sharp teeth, male baboons can be dangerous. However, Joan Silk who worked on one male baboon study says, "They can be sweet with infants."

Baboon dads don't monkey around when they protect their babies. If a baboon baby gets in a fight, Dad rushes to help. Dad's help is **crucial** in keeping his offspring safe. When he is near, his babies are less likely to get hurt.

Silk is thrilled that animal dads act like human dads. She adds, "It's always fun to find out that animals are smarter than you thought!"

# Species in Danger

Animals often must **adjust** to a changing environment. But sometimes animals cannot adapt fast enough to **survive**. If a species, or kind of animal, is in danger of dying out, it is said to be endangered. California has 111 endangered animal species. Here are a few of them.

California condor

Coho salmon

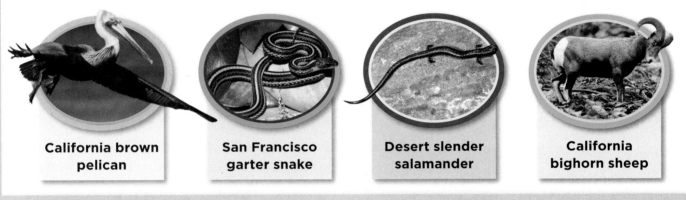

California brown pelican

San Francisco garter snake

Desert slender salamander

California bighorn sheep

# The Frog Finder

It was just after midnight when zoologist Stephen Richards heard a strange whistle. He listened for the odd sound through the patter of rain and then headed toward it.

When he found the **source** of the noise, he gently picked it up. It bit him on the hand! "I was shocked," he says. "Frogs don't normally bite you." Such **unpredictable** behavior was exciting to Richards. That bite, along with the frog's odd cry and appearance, could only mean one thing: He had discovered a new species!

The frog that bit Stephen Richards was a "warty brown blob" found deep in the forest.

LOG ON ▶ Find out more about animals at www.macmillanmh.com.

203

# CALL OF THE WILD

## How do animals react when the environment they live in changes?

Have you ever heard a coyote howl at night? If you have, you may live near coyote country. These days, coyote country is nearly everywhere, but this was not always true. Coyotes used to live mostly in the Great Plains states.

How did this coyote spread occur? Each year, more and more suburban homes are built near coyote country. Since coyotes prefer open land, they roam farther away from old habitats in search of it. Coyotes have been forced to **adjust** to living near humans as open land becomes more difficult to find.

Coyotes are learning to live among humans. This can be dangerous for coyotes.

## Adapting to Survive

Change is good. At least it is for some animals. Over long periods of time, most animals must change as their environment changes. These changes are called adaptations, and they can be **crucial** to an animal's existence.

An Arctic fox has white fur in winter. This helps them blend into the snow.

Arctic foxes, for example, have made several adaptations to the Arctic environment. Thick white fur keeps foxes warm. Its color also helps them blend into the snow and ice. In summer, a fox's fur becomes brown. With the snow gone, brown fur helps the fox almost disappear against the dark ground. These color changes make it harder for enemies to spot the fox.

Another example of adaptation is found in the Galapagos Islands, in the Pacific Ocean. Hundreds of years ago, a type of bird called a finch flew to the islands from South America. The original Galapagos finches had only one type of beak. But over time, some finches developed beaks with different sizes and shapes. The beaks allowed them to eat different types of food found on the islands. Birds with long, thin beaks could get food from a thorny cactus. A finch with a strong beak was able to break open hard seeds. Thanks to these adaptations, the finches continue to thrive on the islands.

Finches on the Galapagos Islands have different types of beaks based on their diet.

## Finding Food

Just as an animal's body may adapt, so can its behavior. Take coyotes, for example. They usually feed on birds, rodents, and small mammals. But coyotes living near humans seek fruits and vegetables from home gardens. They eat pet food left out for dogs or cats. They have even learned how to tip garbage cans to find scraps.

## Animals Gone Wild

Other animals are also learning to adjust to living around people. Wild turkeys have moved into some suburban backyards in Detroit, Michigan. A new **source** of food for them is backyard bird feeders.

Javelinas have eaten their way through many neighborhoods in Phoenix, Arizona. These wild pigs normally live in the desert and eat desert plants. Now they're chowing down on plants found in home gardens.

Black bears have been on the prowl in the suburbs of New Jersey. They have developed a taste for human food—and learned how to get it. Some bears have even climbed tall fences to get to food in a dumpster. The bears threw the food over the fence and climbed back over it. Then they took off with their treats.

This bear is hungry! He is looking for food in his new "neighborhood."

## On the Hot Seat

Another major change to animal environments is caused by global warming. Certain animals now must adjust to Earth's rising temperature. Some birds, fish, and turtles have changed the way they migrate. Some animals migrate, or travel, great distances each year to eat or breed.

Loggerhead turtles have adapted to global warming.

For example, the loggerhead turtle and the little egret bird used to migrate to southern countries in the winter. Now those areas are too warm for them. So they swim and fly to cooler places, closer to the north and south poles. In England, some birds have stopped flying south and are staying put the whole year.

Scientists think this adaptation is a good thing. These changes will help animals live in a warmer climate. Changes to the environment are often **unpredictable**. What is certain is that the animals that adapt to such changes will probably **survive** it.

## CA Critical Thinking

1. What are some of the **causes** that threaten animal survival?

2. Coyotes, bears, and other wild animals are sharing space with humans in the suburbs. Do you think the animals should be removed or allowed to stay? Explain your answer using details from the story.

3. What **effect** is global warming having on some birds and turtles?

4. How does the behavior of baboon fathers help their species survive?

# A WILD Vote

**This African buffalo looks at the camera. Will the herd go after the photographer?**

The African buffaloes agreed to head east. The decision was made quietly. First, several members of the herd gazed into the distance. Other buffaloes noticed where they were looking. Then the whole group took off in that direction.

How did the buffaloes decide where to go? Scientists say they voted! Tim Roper is a scientist from England. He was part of a study of how animals act.

"Most groups of animals have a leader," says Roper. Scientists once thought that an animal group simply follows the leader. This study says that the animal kingdom is more of a democracy.

So how do animals take a vote? It depends on the animal. They don't write on pieces of paper! Voting seems to be based on body language, or movement, or calls.

African buffaloes go in the direction the female buffaloes' gaze. Red deer move when three-fifths of the adults stand up. Whooper swans decide when to fly with head movements. Bees dance to get the swarm going. Among these animals, the ayes have it!

**A red deer stands up and sees if others follow. Then the whole group moves.**

208

Go on ▶

**Directions: Now answer Numbers 1–5. Base your answers on the article "A Wild Vote."**

1. **This article is MOSTLY about**

   A   how groups of animals decide where to go.

   B   how African buffaloes decide where to go.

   C   how two scientists from England studied animals.

   D   how groups of animals play Follow-the-Leader.

2. **Which statement is the author MOST LIKELY to agree with?**

   A   Adult females in any animal group choose the direction.

   B   Animal groups vote only by using movements.

   C   If an animal group votes, then it doesn't have a leader.

   D   This study changes what we know about animal groups.

3. **What will happen if two-fifths of a group of red deer stand up?**

   A   Those standing up will move; the rest will stay where they are.

   B   The group will stay where it is until more deer stand up.

   C   The rest will wait to see whether their leader stands up.

   D   The rest of the group will stand up and start to move.

4. **Reread the example in the first paragraph of the article. What can you CONCLUDE about the several members of the herd that gazed into the distance? What DETAILS support your answer?**

5. **What does the author mean when he says "the animal kingdom is more of a democracy"? Use DETAILS from the article in your answer.**

STOP   209

# ✏️ Write on Demand

**CA** Everyone likes things that help make doing tasks easier. Think about something that helps make your life easier. Now <u>write a story</u> about when something made your life easier.

> Narrative writing tells a story about a personal or fictional experience.

> To figure out if a writing prompt asks for narrative writing, look for clue words, such as <u>tell what happened</u> or <u>write a story</u>.

Below see how one student begins a response to the prompt above.

> The topic sentence tells what the writing is about.

Last weekend my uncle brought his dog robot, Bob, to my house. Bob did not look like a dog at all. He was just a small metal machine with wheels, but what a neat machine! The best part about Bob was that he vacuumed while he moved!

Bob worked like a remote-controlled car. I practiced moving him around. I asked my uncle if Bob could help me clean my room. My uncle said Bob could.

Bob helped me get my room clean quickly. I did have to help him by picking things up from the floor first and telling him how to move. But it was fun!

# Writing Prompt

Respond in writing to the prompt below. Write for

12 minutes. Write as much as you can, as well as you can.

Review the hints below before and after you write.

**CA** Everyone has had to change to adjust to a new situation.

Think about a time when you had to change.

Now write a story about a time when you had to change.

## Writing Hints for Prompts

☑ Read the prompt carefully.

☑ Plan your writing by organizing your ideas in proper sequence.

☑ Support your ideas by telling more about each event or reason.

☑ Use a variety of sentence structures.

☑ Choose words that help others understand what you mean.

☑ Review and edit your writing.

What is the most amazing thing you have ever seen an animal do?

LOG ON ▶ Find out more about animal talents at **www.macmillanmh.com**.

# UNUSUAL ANIMAL TALENTS

conversation    scrambled
interrupted     seized
boasting        rebuild

### ✔ Word Parts

**Prefixes** are word parts that come at the beginning of words and change their meaning. The prefix *re-* means "again."

*rebuild* = build again

# MAX
## THE AMAZING HAMSTER

*by Raymond So*

My pet hamster, Max, is really cool and fun. One day while I was feeding Max, my brother, Marco, came to me with a problem.

"The science fair is next month," he said. "I have to come up with a great project."

"That's easy," I said. "Just build a volcano."

"But everyone makes volcanoes!" he cried. "I want to do something really different."

I could see that our **conversation** about volcanoes was over. I stopped talking, and so did Marco. Finally, I **interrupted** the silence and said, "What about Max? Maybe you could use him for a science project."

"Max!" Marco grinned at us and yelled with delight. "That would be great! Thanks, Mike!"

Marco did some research on hamsters. A few days later, he shared his idea.

"I'm not **boasting**, but I think I've got a really smart project. I'll build a maze. I'll see if Max can go through it faster in the morning or at night. I read that hamsters are more active at night. I think Max will be faster then. Want to help?"

I did! We built a cardboard maze. Then we put a food pellet at one end and Max at the other.

At first, Max started to sway back and forth on his little legs, as if rocking like that would help him figure out what was happening. Then, he smelled the food. Max **scrambled** quickly toward it, knocking down a wall as he hurried along. When he reached the food pellet, he **seized** it in his teeth.

"Max did okay, but the maze fell apart!" I said. "Let's **rebuild** it. I'll get some new cardboard."

We made the maze again. The next morning Marco started timing Max. He timed Max twice a day for two weeks—every morning and every night. It turned out that Marco was right. Max was faster at night than in the morning. That little guy is one amazing hamster!

## Reread for Comprehension

### Monitor Comprehension

**Make Judgments** One way to better understand a story is to **make judgments**. To make a judgment, decide what you think about a character's actions. Use your own experiences to make judgments about the actions. Reread the selection. Use your Judgment Chart to make judgments about the brothers' actions.

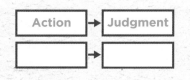

| Action | Judgment |
|--------|----------|
|        |          |

### Genre

**Fantasy** has invented characters who could not exist in real life.

### Monitor Comprehension

**Make Judgments**
As you read, use your Judgment Chart.

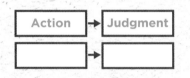

| Action | → | Judgment |
|--------|---|----------|
|        | → |          |

### Read to Find Out

How would you describe Charlotte?

# Wilbur's Boast

## from Charlotte's Web

by E. B. White

illustrated by
Garth Williams

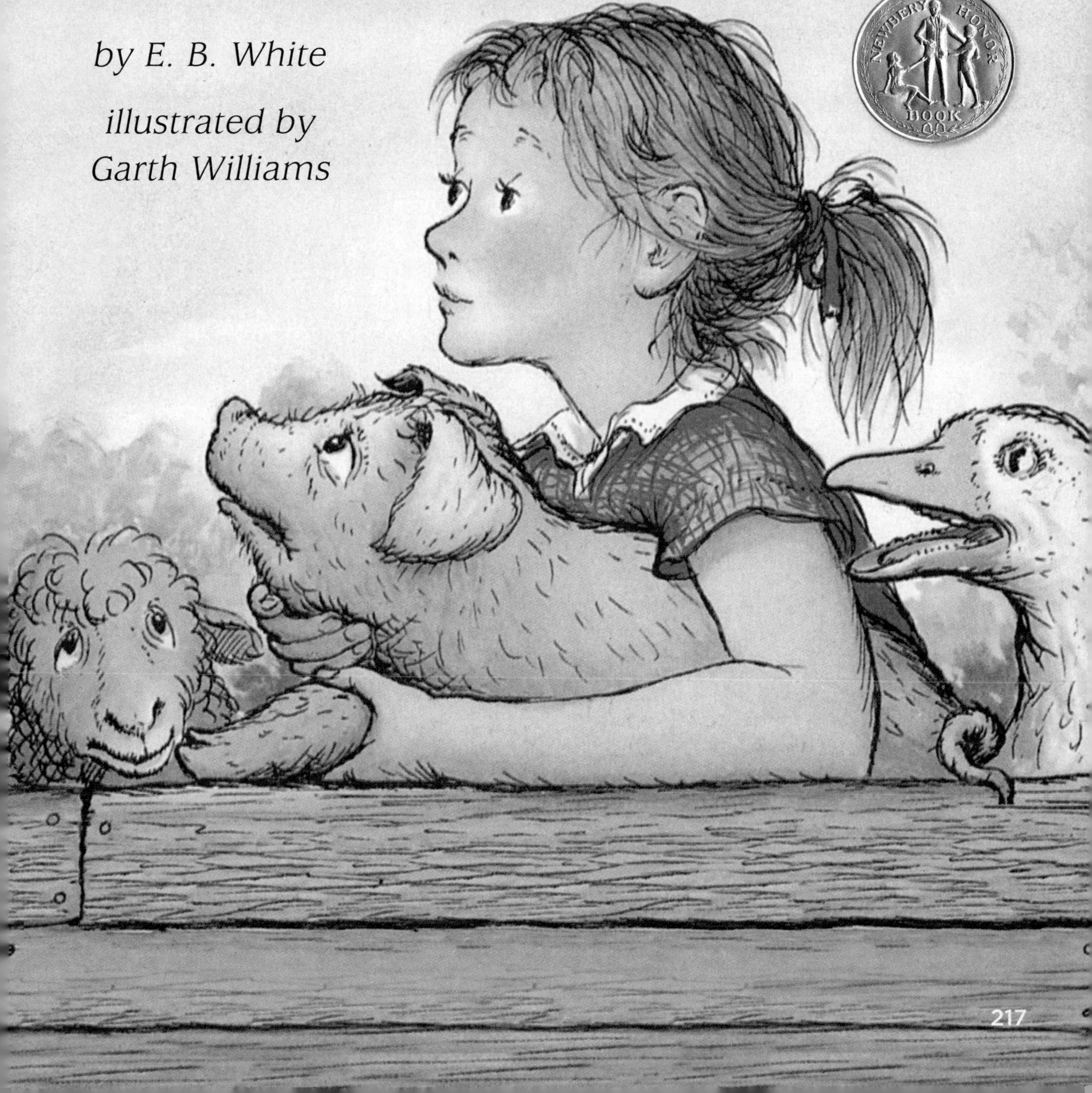

A spider's web is stronger than it looks. Although it is made of thin, delicate strands, the web is not easily broken. However, a web gets torn every day by the insects that kick around in it, and a spider must **rebuild** it when it gets full of holes. Charlotte liked to do her weaving during the late afternoon, and Fern liked to sit nearby and watch. One afternoon she heard a most interesting **conversation** and witnessed a strange event.

"You have awfully hairy legs, Charlotte," said Wilbur, as the spider busily worked at her task.

"My legs are hairy for a good reason," replied Charlotte. "Furthermore, each leg of mine has seven sections—the coxa, the trochanter, the femur, the patella, the tibia, the metatarsus, and the tarsus."

Wilbur sat bolt upright. "You're kidding," he said.

"No, I'm not, either."

"Say those names again, I didn't catch them the first time."

"Coxa, trochanter, femur, patella, tibia, metatarsus, and tarsus."

"Goodness!" said Wilbur, looking down at his own chubby legs. "I don't think *my* legs have seven sections."

---

**Make Judgments**
How do you feel about Wilbur's comment about Charlotte's legs? What kind of manners does Wilbur have?

"Well," said Charlotte, "you and I lead different lives. You don't have to spin a web. That takes real leg work."

"I could spin a web if I tried," said Wilbur, **boasting**. "I've just never tried."

"Let's see you do it," said Charlotte. Fern chuckled softly, and her eyes grew wide with love for the pig.

"O.K.," replied Wilbur. "You coach me and I'll spin one. It must be a lot of fun to spin a web. How do I start?"

"Take a deep breath!" said Charlotte, smiling. Wilbur breathed deeply. "Now climb to the highest place you can get to, like this." Charlotte raced up to the top of the doorway. Wilbur **scrambled** to the top of the manure pile.

"Very good!" said Charlotte. "Now make an attachment with your spinnerets, hurl yourself into space, and let out a dragline as you go down!"

Wilbur hesitated a moment, then jumped out into the air. He glanced hastily behind to see if a piece of rope was following him to check his fall, but nothing seemed to be happening in his rear, and the next thing he knew he landed with a thump. "Ooomp!" he grunted.

Charlotte laughed so hard her web began to sway.

"What did I do wrong?" asked the pig, when he recovered from his bump.

"Nothing," said Charlotte. "It was a nice try."

"I think I'll try again," said Wilbur, cheerfully. "I believe what I need is a little piece of string to hold me."

The pig walked out to his yard. "You there, Templeton?" he called. The rat poked his head out from under the trough.

"Got a little piece of string I could borrow?" asked Wilbur. "I need to spin a web."

"Yes, indeed," replied Templeton, who saved string. "No trouble at all. Anything to oblige." He crept down into his hole, pushed the goose egg out of the way, and returned with an old piece of dirty white string. Wilbur examined it.

"That's just the thing," he said. "Tie one end to my tail, will you, Templeton?"

Wilbur crouched low, with his thin, curly tail toward the rat. Templeton **seized** the string, passed it around the end of the pig's tail, and tied two half hitches. Charlotte watched in delight. Like Fern, she was truly fond of Wilbur, whose smelly pen and stale food attracted the flies that she needed, and she was proud to see that he was not a quitter and was willing to try again to spin a web.

While the rat and the spider and the little girl watched, Wilbur climbed again to the top of the manure pile, full of energy and hope.

"Everybody watch!" he cried. And summoning all his strength, he threw himself into the air, headfirst. The string trailed behind him. But as he had neglected to fasten the other end to anything, it didn't really do any good, and Wilbur landed with a thud, crushed and hurt. Tears came to his eyes. Templeton grinned. Charlotte just sat quietly. After a bit she spoke.

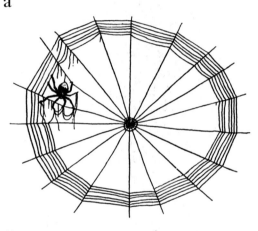

"You can't spin a web, Wilbur, and I advise you to put the idea out of your mind. You lack two things needed for spinning a web."

"What are they?" asked Wilbur, sadly.

"You lack a set of spinnerets, and you lack knowhow. But cheer up, you don't need a web. Zuckerman supplies you with three big meals a day. Why should you worry about trapping food?"

Wilbur sighed. "You're ever so much cleverer and brighter than I am, Charlotte. I guess I was just trying to show off. Serves me right."

Templeton untied his string and took it back to his home. Charlotte returned to her weaving.

"You needn't feel too badly, Wilbur," she said. "Not many creatures can spin webs. Even men aren't as good at it as spiders, although they *think* they're pretty good, and they'll *try* anything. Did you ever hear of the Queensborough Bridge?"

Wilbur shook his head. "Is it a web?"

"Sort of," replied Charlotte. "But do you know how long it took men to build it? Eight whole years. My goodness, I would have starved to death waiting that long. I can make a web in a single evening."

"What do people catch in the Queensborough Bridge—bugs?" asked Wilbur.

"No," said Charlotte. "They don't catch anything. They just keep trotting back and forth across the bridge thinking there is something better on the other side. If they'd hang head-down at the top of the thing and wait quietly, maybe something good would come along. But no—with men it's rush, rush, rush, every minute. I'm glad I'm a sedentary spider."

"What does sedentary mean?" asked Wilbur.

"Means I sit still a good part of the time and don't go wandering all over creation. I know a good thing when I see it, and my web is a good thing. I stay put and wait for what comes. Gives me a chance to think."

"Well, I'm sort of sedentary myself, I guess," said the pig. "I have to hang around here whether I want to or not. You know where I'd really like to be this evening?"

"Where?"

"In a forest looking for beechnuts and truffles and delectable roots, pushing leaves aside with my wonderful strong nose, searching and sniffing along the ground, smelling, smelling, smelling …"

"You smell just the way you are," remarked a lamb who had just walked in. "I can smell you from here. You're the smelliest creature in the place."

Wilbur hung his head. His eyes grew wet with tears. Charlotte noticed his embarrassment and she spoke sharply to the lamb.

"Let Wilbur alone!" she said. "He has a perfect right to smell, considering his surroundings. You're no bundle of sweet peas yourself. Furthermore, you are interrupting a very pleasant conversation. What were we talking about, Wilbur, when we were so rudely **interrupted**?"

"Oh, I don't remember," said Wilbur. "It doesn't make any difference. Let's not talk any more for a while, Charlotte. I'm getting sleepy. You go ahead and finish fixing your web and I'll just lie here and watch you. It's a lovely evening." Wilbur stretched out on his side.

Twilight settled over Zuckerman's barn, and a feeling of peace.

**Make Judgments**
How do you know that Charlotte wants to make Wilbur feel better? What judgment can you make about her?

# Spin a Web with
# E. B. and Garth

### AUTHOR

**E. B. White** had a farm very much like the one in this story. One day when E. B. was going to feed his pig, he began to feel sad. He did not want his pig to be killed. E. B. thought about how to save him. While he was thinking, he saw a big spider spinning a web. Soon E. B. was spinning the novel *Charlotte's Web*.

**Other books** by E. B. White: *Stuart Little* and *The Trumpet of the Swan*

### ILLUSTRATOR

**Garth Williams** has said that *Charlotte's Web* was one of his favorite books to illustrate. Garth did the pictures while he was living on a farm. He based his illustrations on what he saw around him. He drew the animals over and over again until they seemed to look like people.

**LOG ON** ▶ Find out more about E. B. White and Garth Williams at **www.macmillanmh.com**.

### CA Author's Purpose

What was E. B. White's purpose for writing this story? How do you know?

# CA Critical Thinking

## Summarize

Use your Judgment Chart to help you summarize *Wilbur's Boast.* Tell about a character's action in the story and make a judgment about it. Use story information and your own experience.

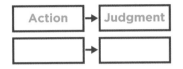

| Action | → | Judgment |
|--------|---|----------|
|        | → |          |

## Think and Compare

1. **Make a judgment** about Wilbur's **boasting**. Why is spinning a web a good or bad idea for Wilbur? Explain. Include story details in your answer. **Monitor Comprehension: Make Judgments**

2. Reread page 225. How does Charlotte feel about humans? Why does she feel her life is better? Use story details and information in your answer. **Evaluate**

3. Suppose you could meet Charlotte. What would you ask her about the meaning of friendship? **Apply**

4. Why does Charlotte explain to Wilbur how to spin a web? **Analyze**

5. Read "Max, the Amazing Hamster" on pages 214–215. Compare Max with the animals in *Wilbur's Boast.* Which story is more realistic? Use details from both selections to explain your answer. **Reading/Writing Across Texts**

**Fables** teach a lesson and often have animal characters that talk and act like people.

## ✦ Literary Elements

**Personification** is when an animal or thing is given human characteristics.

A **Moral** is the lesson a fable teaches. The reader can apply it to his or her own personal experiences.

# THE LION AND THE MOUSE

*retold by Max McGee*

More than anything else in the world, Lion liked being King of the Jungle. He strutted all around, showing off his impressive, shaggy mane.

Each day Lion took a long, lazy nap under the shade of his favorite tree. He always dreamed of weaker jungle creatures bowing before him.

One day Mouse scurried through the jungle and tripped over Lion's huge paws.

Lion woke up with a start. "How dare you wake me up!" he roared furiously.

Lion grabbed Mouse with one paw. "On second thought, I'm in the mood for a snack, and you'll make a delicious morsel," he said.

Mouse cried out, "King Lion, please spare me! If you let me live, I will always remember your kindness. And, some day, I might be able to help you."

**A mouse who speaks and thinks is an example of personification.**

"How could such a powerless little mouse ever help me?" That thought made Lion laugh so much that he decided to let Mouse go. A week later, Lion was strutting through the jungle on the way to his napping tree when he stepped onto a hunter's net. The net scooped him up. No matter how he twisted and turned, he couldn't escape.

When Mouse heard Lion's frightened roars, he raced to help. Mouse quickly chewed through the ropes to make a hole in the net. Soon, Lion crawled out and was free.

Lion looked down at the little mouse. "Thank you for saving my life," said Lion, smiling his widest smile. "I was mistaken. You are not a powerless little mouse. You are a great friend!"

Moral: *Even the small can show great strength.*

## CA Critical Thinking

1. How are Lion's actions like those of a real person's? Use details from the story in your answer. **Personification**

2. How do Mouse's actions help you understand the fable's moral? **Analyze**

3. Compare the mouse in this fable with Charlotte in *Wilbur's Boast*. How are they similar? How are they different? **Reading/Writing Across Texts**

LOG ON ▶ Find out more about fables at www.macmillanmh.com.

# Reading and Writing Connection

**Distinguishing Moments**

Good writers use many details to describe an important moment. This helps readers experience it.

Read the passage below. Notice how author E. B. White describes one moment in great detail.

**An excerpt from**
*Wilbur's Boast*

The author uses many details when telling about the moment Wilbur jumped, so that we can picture exactly what was happening at that time.

"Everybody watch!" he cried. And summoning all his strength, he threw himself into the air, headfirst. The string trailed behind him. But as he had neglected to fasten the other end to anything, it didn't really do any good, and Wilbur landed with a thud, crushed and hurt. Tears came to his eyes. Templeton grinned. Charlotte just sat quietly.

# Read and Find

Read Mike's writing below. How did he show exactly what was happening in the moment? Use the Writer's Checklist to help you.

## Mike's Ball Game
### By Mike T.

I stood in front of the tall shrubs holding my baseball glove above my eyes to block the sun. The sweat fell into my eyes as I looked towards home plate. My cousin hit a long shot. I thought the ball was going to fly over my head. I set my feet and reached my glove up. The ball sailed into my glove.

Read about when I played in a ball game.

# Writer's Checklist

 Does the author show us exactly what was happening when he made the catch?

 Does the author show how one event caused another event to happen in that one moment?

 Does it feel as if you are watching what happened?

233

# Survival and
# Adaptation

**Talk About It**

How has this animal adapted to its environment?

LOG ON ▶ Find out more about survival and adaptation at **www.macmillanmh.com**.

235

# What Curious Creatures!

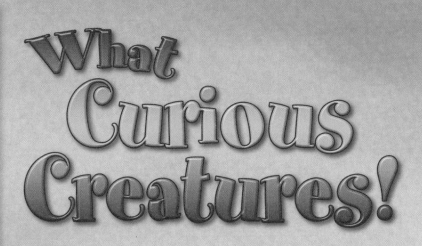

The world is full of unusual animals. Things that make an animal unusual and special include where it lives and how it looks. One animal with a special look is a lion, which is a kind of cat. Lions look similar to house cats because they are **related** to each other. But they are different from each other in important ways. House cats can be pets, but lions live in the wild.

Sometimes male and **female** animals look exactly alike. In other ways they are not **identical**. With lions, the male lion has a thick mane, or hair, around its head. Female lions do not have this. On the other hand, the same kind of male and female house cat may look alike.

Some special qualities of animals are not clear at first **sight**. One example of this is how an animal protects itself. What an animal uses to protect itself cannot always be seen. Some animals, such as snakes, use poison called **venom**. A snake passes venom onto another creature through its bite. Another protection animals can use is **odor**. Skunks, for example, spray a strong smell to keep animals away.

Many people enjoy studying all the things that make animals special. Different kinds of animals live in forests, deserts, the ocean, and in cold areas. Wherever people live, unusual animals can be found there, too.

## Reread for Comprehension

### Summarize

**Compare and Contrast** When you **compare** two or more people, things, or events, you look for ways that they are alike, or similar. When you look for ways that they are different, you **contrast** them. A Venn diagram helps you summarize what you've read so you can compare and contrast the information. Reread the article to compare and contrast the different kinds of animals.

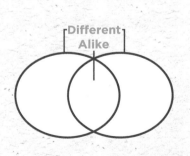

237

**Comprehension**

### Genre

Nonfiction articles give information about real people, places, or things.

### Summarize

Compare and Contrast As you read, use your Venn diagram.

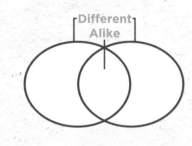

Different
Alike

### Read to Find Out

What unique animals live in the deserts of the Southwest?

# Unique Animals

## By Tanya Lee Stone

# INTRODUCTION

There are four major deserts in the Southwest region. Parts of the Chihuahuan Desert fall in Texas and New Mexico. The Sonoran Desert covers almost half of Arizona. Part of the Mojave Desert crosses into Nevada. And the Great Basin Desert blankets a huge part of Nevada.

A variety of wildlife lives in these deserts, and in the rest of the Southwest region. Some of these animals are especially well known.

A variety of unique animals, including the Gila monster, make their home in the American Southwest.

240

This peccary makes its home in the American Southwest.

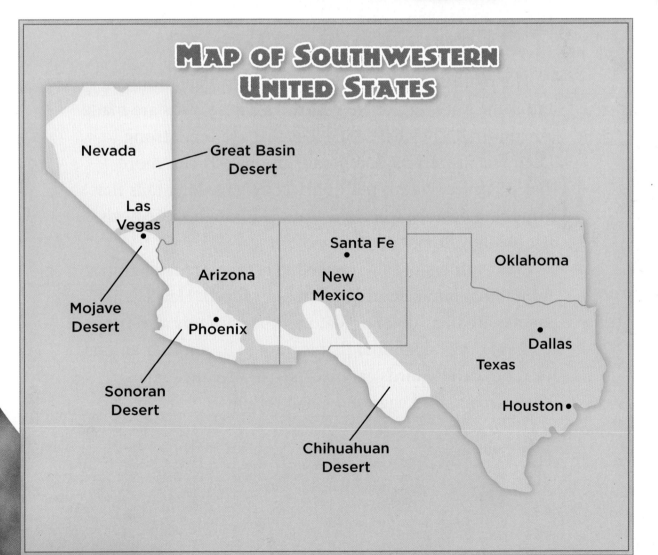

## MAP OF SOUTHWESTERN UNITED STATES

Nevada

Great Basin Desert

Las Vegas

Mojave Desert

Arizona

Santa Fe

New Mexico

Oklahoma

Phoenix

Dallas

Texas

Sonoran Desert

Chihuahuan Desert

Houston

# Racing Around!

The roadrunner is a common **sight** in the Southwest and is the state bird of New Mexico. These birds are made for running! They have long legs that are very strong. Their feet are strong, too. Roadrunners can run more than 15 miles (24km) per hour! They have long tails that help them balance when they run. Although these birds can fly, they do not do it very often.

Roadrunners use their speed to escape predators (an animal that hunts another animal for food). Hawks and coyotes are their main predators. Roadrunners also run to chase prey (an animal that is hunted by another animal for food). These birds eat insects, lizards, and snakes. They also eat bird eggs and small rodents.

In addition to being fast runners, roadrunners are able to hop around and change direction quickly. This helps confuse or tire another animal. Roadrunners use this trick on rattlesnakes. As soon as the snake gets tired from trying to strike at the roadrunner, the bird stabs the snake with its strong beak. Roadrunners are so fast on their feet they can even snatch a hummingbird or dragonfly that flies too close!

**Roadrunners have long tails that help them balance when they run.**

# ARMORED ARMADILLOS

Armadillos are **related** to sloths and anteaters. The nine-banded armadillo is the state mammal of Texas. It is also found in Oklahoma and in southern states east of Texas. Armadillos are mainly nocturnal. This means they sleep during the day and are active at night. They sometimes search for food in the daytime. They eat ants, beetles, and termites. Their sharp sense of smell helps them find food. They use their long, sticky tongues to pull ants and termites from their nests. Armadillos eat other kinds of insects, too. They also feed on fruit, bird eggs, snakes, and carrion (dead animals).

The armadillo uses its sharp sense of smell to find ants, beetles, and termites.

An armadillo is about 18 to 22 inches (46 to 56cm) long. Its tail adds an extra 9 to 15 inches (23 to 38cm). It has a long, pointy nose and large, pointy ears. Armadillos are born with soft, leathery skin. As they grow, their skin starts to harden. They develop bony plates that cover most of their bodies.

This bony plating is used for protection. When it is in danger, an armadillo can curl up. That way, its soft belly stays safe. This protects it from enemies. Armadillos also use speed to escape enemies. They slip into burrows to hide when necessary. Armadillos use their strong legs and claws to dig burrows more than six feet (2m) deep and 15 feet (5m) long. Burrows are used for sleeping, escaping danger, and nesting. Nine-banded armadillos are the only mammals that give birth to four **identical** babies.

**Compare and Contrast**
Compare and contrast the ways in which armadillos and roadrunners protect themselves.

Armadillos curl into a ball to protect their soft belly when they sense danger.

Collared peccaries are a common sight throughout the Southwest. This mammal looks like a pig, but belongs to its own family. They are 35 to 45 inches (89 to 114cm) long. They weigh 30 to 60 pounds (14 to 27 kg). A collared peccary gets its name from the band of fur around its neck. It is also called a javelina or a musk hog.

Smell plays a big part in this animal's life. It gives off a strong **odor** and can be smelled from a few hundred feet away. It is also good at using its nose to find other members of its herd. These animals usually live in groups of twelve to fifteen. They have a scent gland on their backs. This is used to mark territory.

**A collared peccary uses its excellent sense of smell to sniff out its favorite foods.**

Collared peccaries also use their excellent sense of smell to find food. They can sniff out roots several inches under the ground. They eat roots, herbs, nuts, berries, and grasses. They also feed on fruit and worms. One of their favorite foods is the prickly pear cactus.

**Female** collared peccaries usually give birth to two babies. The whole herd helps look out for the young. A baby can travel with the herd when it is only a day old. These animals can run fast—up to 25 miles (40km) per hour! They usually choose to run from a predator. They will also make noises to alert the rest of the herd. If it has to, a collared peccary will use its sharp teeth on an enemy. A collared peccary can even fight off a bobcat or coyote.

Baby collared peccaries can keep up with their mothers a day after their birth.

# CUNNING COYOTES

A coyote is a medium-sized member of the dog family. It is related to the wolf, but is much smaller. It has pointy ears and a droopy, bushy tail. Its tail is about as long as its body. Coyotes can be found in most parts of North America. But these wild dogs are a common sight in the Southwest. They even live in neighborhoods and cities.

Like all wild dogs, coyotes communicate with each other through sounds. Coyotes howl, bark, whine, and growl. In fact, scientists have discovered that coyotes make many different sounds. Different sounds have different meanings, such as "danger" or "keep out!" Coyotes also communicate with each other by moving their ears and tails different ways.

A coyote howls for its pack. Coyotes howl, whine, and growl to communicate with each other.

A coyote feasts on a rodent

Coyotes hunt alone, in pairs, or in a small group. They have keen hearing and an excellent sense of smell. A coyote can run up to 40 miles (64km) per hour. They are great swimmers and can leap up to 13 feet (4m). All of these things make coyotes good hunters. They will eat almost anything, but seem to prefer small mammals such as mice, rats, rabbits, and squirrels. They also eat carrion, fruits, and vegetables.

Coyotes often mate for life. The female usually gives birth to her pups inside a safe, cozy den. Coyotes either build their own dens or take over the home of another animal. A coyote pair raises its young together. Pups are born blind, and with floppy ears. Within about ten days, their ears start to stand up and they are able to see.

These coyotes hunt together for their favorite foods but will eat almost anything.

# Raccoon Relatives

Ringtails and coatis are both related to raccoons and both live in the Southwest. The ringtail is Arizona's state mammal. It is also found in Nevada, Oklahoma, Texas, and New Mexico. A ringtail is about the size of a house cat. It gets its name from its long, bushy tail that has black and white rings.

Ringtails are nocturnal. They sleep most of the day in small spaces such as rock crevices and hollow logs. At night, they hunt. They are expert climbers and have excellent hearing and eyesight. This makes them good hunters. Ringtails eat small mammals, lizards, frogs, and birds. They also eat snakes, insects, and fruit.

The ringtail hunts at night

White-nosed coatis also eat both plants and animals. They like fruits, nuts, insects, and eggs. They also eat rodents, lizards, and snakes. Coatis eat carrion, too.

As its name suggests, the white-nosed coati has a white snout. Unlike ringtails, the coati is a diurnal animal. This means it sleeps at night and is active during the day. Like ringtails, white-nosed coatis are good climbers. Their long tails help them balance while in trees.

The coati looks for food during the day. Both ringtails and coatis are excellent climbers.

**Compare and Contrast**
Compare and contrast ringtails and coatis.

# DESERT DIGGERS

A tortoise is a type of turtle that lives on land. The desert tortoise is the state reptile of Nevada. It is a threatened species. That means it is against the law to harm them. Desert tortoises can live up to 80 years if left alone! Reptiles such as the tortoise are cold-blooded animals. This means that the temperature of their bodies changes with the temperature of the air around them.

Desert tortoises live in both the Sonoran and Mojave deserts. They are able to live in areas where temperatures on the ground reach 140 degrees Fahrenheit (60 degrees Celsius)! Desert tortoises live in underground burrows to escape the heat. Sometimes they look for shade under big rocks. Their burrows also protect them from cold temperatures in the winter. In fact, desert tortoises spend most of their lives in their burrows.

**Desert tortoises are cold-blooded animals that can live to eighty years old.**

Desert tortoises weigh about 8 to 15 pounds (4 to 7kg). Their carapace (top shell) is 9 to 15 inches (23 to 38cm) long. These tortoises have strong front limbs for digging. They use them to dig burrows. Desert tortoises also dig shallow basins to catch rainwater. They remember where the basins are and return to them when it rains. These tortoises are plant eaters. They get some of the water they need from the grasses and wildflowers they eat. If necessary, a desert tortoise can live a year without water.

Tortoises are plant eaters. Here, a tortoise nibbles on grasses in its path.

A collared lizard eats its prey. Collared lizards hunt mostly in the cooler morning and late afternoon hours.

# Leapin' Lizards!

The Southwest is home to many kinds of lizards. The collared lizard is Oklahoma's state reptile. It is also found in other states of this region. Other common lizards throughout the Southwest include the chuckwalla and the Gila monster.

Collared lizards are diurnal, but are mostly active in the morning or late afternoon when it is not as hot. They are swift runners. They sometimes stand upright on their back legs when they run. Males often sit on high rocks where they have a good view of the area. This may be to guard the territory, watch for females, or spot prey. Collared lizards mostly eat insects and other small lizards.

Chuckwallas are herbivores. A chuckwalla likes flowers, leaves, and buds. Chuckwallas have a unique way of protecting themselves from predators. They have folds of loose skin on their flat bodies. To escape danger, a chuckwalla will crawl into a small space such as a crack in a ledge. It then gulps air and puffs up its body so it becomes wedged into place. It is practically impossible to get a chuckwalla out until it is good and ready to come out!

A Gila monster does not need much protection. It is one of only two venomous lizards in the world. It is a beaded lizard. Its rounded scales look a lot like beads. Gila monsters are big and colorful. They have strong claws made for digging. These reptiles spend hot desert days under rocks or in holes they dig. They come out at dusk to hunt. Gila monsters move slowly, except when striking prey. A Gila monster will clamp its jaws onto a small mammal or bird quickly. Its **venom** then flows into the animal's wound and kills it.

# Serious Snakes!

Snakes are reptiles. They are cold-blooded animals. When they need to cool their bodies down, they look for shade. When they need to warm up, they bask in the sun. Many different kinds of snakes live in the Southwest. Some are poisonous and some are not.

Coral snakes and rattlesnakes are particularly dangerous. Coral snakes are very colorful. They have red, yellow, and black bands. Other snakes with similar colors are not poisonous, so it is important to be able to tell them apart. One easy way is to remember the saying, "red touches yellow—deadly fellow." This refers to the coral snake. Their coloring warns off predators. Coral snakes use their venom to kill prey. They mainly eat lizards and other kinds of snakes.

**A coral snake uses its powerful venom to kill another snake**

There are many different kinds of rattlesnakes, but they all have jointed rattles at the ends of their tails. Each time a rattlesnake molts (sheds its skin) a new piece of the rattle is formed. Rattlesnakes shake their rattles when they are threatened.

A rattlesnake is a pit viper. This kind of snake has two large pits in its head. The pits are heat-sensing organs. This helps a rattlesnake find its prey. Rattlesnakes also pick up nearby scents with their flickering tongues. A rattlesnake will strike its victim and inject the animal with its venom. Rattlesnakes eat small mammals, lizards, and even birds. A western diamondback can even swallow an animal that outweighs it!

Scorpions are found on every continent except Antarctica. They are well suited to the desert and are common in the Southwest. Several different kinds of scorpions live in this region. Scorpions are arachnids and have four pairs of legs. They also have two pincer claws.

A scorpion has a sharp stinger on the end of its tail. This stinger packs a punch—it comes with poison glands! A scorpion warns off predators with its poisonous stinger. It also uses the venom to kill its prey. Scorpions eat spiders, insects, and other scorpions! A scorpion attacks by swinging its tail up over its body and plunging its stinger into the prey. The most poisonous scorpion in the United States—the bark scorpion—makes its home in Arizona. It is quite dangerous to humans.

A mother scorpion carries her babies on her back

This scorpion (below) used the poisonous stinger on its tail to kill a beetle for its lunch.

Tarantulas live in many parts of the Southwest. They are arachnids, too. Their eight legs are hairy! Although they have eight eyes, they still cannot see very well. Tarantulas are the largest spiders in the world. Their bodies are 1 to 3 inches (2.54 to 8cm) long. Tarantulas are generally not poisonous to people. But these spiders have poison glands inside their jaws. The glands are connected to two pointed fangs. When it senses an insect nearby, a tarantula runs quickly to it and stabs it with its fangs. The poison kills the insect and the spider can begin its meal.

There are many unique and wonderful animals that live in the Southwest region. They all add to the area's richness and beauty.

# THE UNIQUE TANYA LEE STONE

Author **Tanya Lee Stone** likes to write fiction and nonfiction for children. Ever since she was a child, she loved creating stories. Going to school and helping other people write children's stories helped her grow as a writer. She has published close to 80 books for children and teens. When she's not writing, she likes to visit schools and talk to students about writing and how research is important.

Tanya Lee Stone

**Another book** by Tanya Lee Stone

WILD AMERICA
MOUSE

LOG ON ▶ Find out more about Tanya Lee Stone at **www.macmillanmh.com**.

## (CA) Author's Purpose

What was Tanya Lee Stone's purpose for writing Unique Animals of the Southwest? What details from the article help you to understand the author's purpose?

# CA Critical Thinking

## Summarize

Use your Venn diagram to help you summarize *Unique Animals of the Southwest.* Describe how the animals in the Southwest are alike and different.

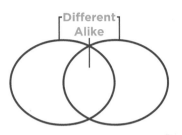

## Think and Compare

1. **Compare and contrast** the ways roadrunners and snakes find their food. **Summarize: Compare and Contrast**

2. Reread about collared peccaries on pages 246–247. How is this animal's sense of smell important? Include details in your answer. **Analyze**

3. In what ways are coyotes similar to pet dogs? How are they different? **Evaluate**

4. Many animals look for someplace safe at the first **sight** of danger. Some depend on sounds and smells. How do sounds and smells help keep you safe? **Apply**

5. Read "What Curious Creatures!" on pages 236–237. How is this selection similar to *Unique Animals of the Southwest*? How are they different? Use details from both selections in your answer. **Reading/Writing Across Texts**

**Genre**

**Myths** are stories that people used to explain how certain things in the world came to be.

✔ **Literary Elements**

**Foreshadowing** is the use of clues to hint at what is going to happen later in a story.

# The Story of the First Woodpecker

## by Florence Holbrook

IN THE DAYS OF LONG AGO, the Great Spirit would come down from the sky. Once, as he went up and down the earth, he came to the wigwam of a woman. He went into the wigwam and sat down by the fire, but he looked like an old man, and the woman did not know who he was.

"I have fasted for many days," said the Great Spirit to the woman. "Will you give me some food?" The woman made a very little cake and put it into the fire. "You can have this cake," she said, "if you will wait for it to bake." "I will wait," he said.

When the cake was baked, the woman stood and looked at it. She thought, "it is very large. I thought it small. I will not give him so large a cake as that." So she put it away and made a small one. "If you will wait, I will give you this when it is baked," she said, and the Great Spirit said, "I will wait."

When that cake was baked, it was larger than the first one. "It is so large that I will keep it for a feast," she thought. So she said to her guest, "I will not give you this cake, but if you will wait, I will make you another one." "I will wait," said the Great Spirit again.

Then the woman made another cake. It was smaller than the others had been at first, but when she went to the fire for it, she found it the largest of all. She did not know that the Great Spirit's magic had made each cake larger, and she thought, "This is a marvel, but I will not give away the largest cake of all." So she said to her guest, "I have no food for you. Go to the forest and look there for your food. You can find it in the bark of the trees, if you will."

The woman bakes two cakes and does not give them to the man. This foreshadows that she might do the same with the third cake.

The Great Spirit was angry when he heard the words of the woman. He rose up from where he sat and threw back his cloak. "People must be good and gentle," he said, "and you are cruel. You shall no longer be a woman and live in a wigwam. You shall go out into the forests and hunt for your food in the bark of trees."

The Great Spirit stamped his foot on the earth, and the woman grew smaller and smaller. Wings started from her body and feathers grew upon her. With a loud cry she rose from the earth and flew away to the forest.

And to this day all woodpeckers live in the forest and hunt for their food in the bark of trees.

 **Critical Thinking**

1. What is another example of foreshadowing in this myth? **Foreshadowing**

2. Why is it important to know that the woman did not know who the old man really is? **Analyze**

3. This myth tells about why a woodpecker must look for food in a certain way. Compare and contrast how different animals gather food in *Unique Animals of the Southwest*. **Reading/Writing Across Texts**

 Find out more about foreshadowing at **www.macmillanmh.com**.

## Writing

### ✓ Distinguishing Moments

Writing about an important moment can give details about a certain event, person, place, or thing.

# Reading and Writing Connection

Read the passage below. Notice what author Tanya Lee Stone tells us by describing an important moment in the life of a rattlesnake.

**An excerpt from**
*Unique Animals of the Southwest*

The author tells about the moment a rattlesnake finds its prey, so you can understand this particular snake's eating habits.

A rattlesnake is a pit viper. This kind of snake has two large pits in its head. The pits are heat-sensing organs. This helps a rattlesnake find its prey. Rattlesnakes also pick up nearby scents with their flickering tongues. A rattlesnake will strike its victim and inject the animal with its venom. Rattlesnakes eat small mammals, lizards, and even birds. A western diamondback can even swallow an animal that outweighs it!

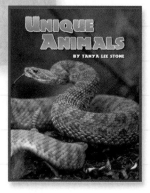

UNIQUE ANIMALS
BY TANYA LEE STONE

# Read and Find

How does Billy describe one daily moment and provide us with details about feeding goldfish? Use the Writer's Checklist to help you.

# Goldfish

### By Billy S.

My goldfish has been alive for three months. I feed it every day. I sprinkle a few flakes over the bowl and watch to see if my goldfish will come to eat. I see it swim up close to the surface to eat the flakes of food. Its lips pucker as it gets close to the flake. Then it gobbles a flake and dives around the bowl.

Read about when I feed my goldfish.

# Writer's Checklist

 Does the author show us what happens when he feeds his pet?

✓ Does the author show how one event causes another event to happen?

☑ Does it feel as if you are watching it happen?

## Review

Cause and Effect
Sequence
Draw Conclusions
Homophones
Directions

# JOSH'S DISCOVERY

"Today we're going to take a hike in the desert," said Ms. Fogerty, Marcia's teacher. Marcia was excited to go on a field trip with her class. She loved being outside and exploring new places.

Marcia's friend Josh wasn't as excited. "The desert is nothing but sand and the hot sun," he said. "I'd rather stay here for art class." Josh loved art.

The class got on the bus. Soon they were driving out of the city into an area where there were just a few houses. After about 40 minutes, they saw a sign for Red Rock Canyon Scenic Drive. "This is it!" cried Ms. Fogerty.

Once the bus turned, the class saw hikers and bikers moving along the road. After a few minutes, Ms. Fogerty instructed the bus driver, "Pull over here, please. This is our trail."

"Remember, you'll write a report on what you see here today. Keep your eyes open and be alert," said Ms. Fogerty.

"What are we supposed to be looking at?" Josh asked.

Ms. Fogerty replied, "Look all around you. Since it is spring, some of the cactuses are in bloom. If we're lucky, we'll see desert wildflowers farther down the trail. You might see some animals, too. Maybe you'll see lizards, birds, or even snakes!"

"I bet we won't see anything that interesting," said Josh quietly to Marcia. She gave him a mean look.

After walking a few minutes, Marcia yelled, "Look! A rabbit!" The students oohed and aahed as the rabbit hopped away. Josh stayed silent.

Then another student called out, "Check out this cactus. It looks like an old man's beard!" There were laughs and more oohs and aahs. Josh was still silent.

The children kept calling out their discoveries. Josh didn't say anything. Then he noticed something on a tall group of rocks. There were pictures—wavy lines, stick men, four-legged animals. "What are these?" Josh asked Ms. Fogerty.

"Those are petroglyphs. Some people call them rock art. Native Americans who lived here hundreds of years ago made them. No one is sure what the pictures mean."

"Now that's something to write about!" said Josh happily.

"I guess the desert isn't so bad after all," said Marcia, as the children drove home on the bus.

"Bad?" asked Josh. "No, it's amazing!"

# TORNADOES

## Nature's Toughest Storms

### What Is a Tornado?

A tornado is a funnel of wind spinning very fast. Its wind can blow as fast as 300 miles per hour, which is almost six times the speed limit on a highway! Tornadoes can be caused by powerful thunderstorms called supercells. Cold, dry air mixing with warm, moist air makes a supercell. When the warm air in the supercell rises very quickly, it starts to spin into a tornado.

When a tornado reaches the ground, it begins to travel. A tornado can have a straight, a zigzag, or a circular path. The damage along this path can be as wide as 1 or 2 miles and as long as 50 miles. Tornadoes typically touch down for only two or three minutes.

At first a tornado's long cone shape is almost invisible. As it picks up dirt and other materials, the tornado gets darker and becomes easier to see. A tornado can also pick up cars, trees, and parts of buildings.

**Staying Safe in a Tornado**

Tornadoes are hard to predict, but meteorologists can help with this. Be sure to listen to local weather warnings. Also, the sky might appear slightly greenish just before a tornado. Loud winds that sound like a train might mean a tornado is very close.

The best place to take cover from a tornado is in a place without windows, such as a cellar, hallway, or closet. People in cars should stop driving and get into a building as quickly as possible.

Tornadoes come in different shapes and sizes.

---

**Tornado Safety Directions**

**At school**

1. Go to an interior hall or room in an orderly way.
2. Crouch low, keep your head down.
3. Protect the back of your head with your arms.
4. Stay away from windows and large open rooms, such as gyms.

**In a car or bus**

1. Drive out of its path, if possible. If not, go to Step 2.
2. Park the car quickly and safely.
3. Get out and seek shelter in a sturdy building.
4. If in the open country, run to low ground, away from any cars.
5. Crouch low, keep your head down.
6. Protect the back of your head with your arms.

# CA Critical Thinking

**Now answer Numbers 1 through 4. Base your answers on the passage "Josh's Discovery."**

**1. What happens FIRST in the passage?**

   **A**   The children see a cactus.

   **B**   Marcia sees a rabbit.

   **C**   Josh sees petroglyphs.

   **D**   Ms. Fogerty tells the children that they're going to the desert.

**2. Why is Josh silent during the hike?**

   **A**   He does not think the trip is as much fun as art class.

   **B**   He is too excited to speak.

   **C**   He is angry at Marcia.

   **D**   He is jealous of another class that is taking a different trip.

**3. Read this sentence from the story.**

> Marcia was excited to go on a field trip with her class. She loved being outside and exploring new places.

**Which of the following words from this sentence could be spelled differently and have a different meaning?**

   **A**   go

   **B**   trip

   **C**   class

   **D**   new

**4. What causes Josh to change his mind about the desert? Use details from the passage to support your answer.**

Now answer Numbers 1 through 4. Base your answers on the passage "Tornadoes: Nature's Toughest Storms."

**1.** **What might you see BEFORE a tornado arrives?**

    **A**  scampering animals

    **B**  snow

    **C**  cars stalling on the roads

    **D**  a greenish sky

**2.** **Based on the passage, what conclusion can you draw about the speed of a tornado?**

    **A**  All tornadoes have winds of over 200 miles per hour.

    **B**  Most tornadoes can outrun a car.

    **C**  Tornadoes slow down after they travel for 50 miles.

    **D**  Many tornadoes travel at the speed of light.

**3.** **A tornado is caused by**

    **A**  cold, moist air mixing with warm, moist air.

    **B**  high air mixing with low air.

    **C**  windy air mixing with a supercell.

    **D**  cold, dry air mixing with warm, moist air.

**4.** **According to "Tornado Safety Directions," which step is the same whether you're in a car or at school?**

    **A**  Get out and seek shelter in a sturdy building.

    **B**  Drive out of its path, if possible.

    **C**  Protect the back of your head with your arms.

    **D**  Run to low ground, away from any cars.

## Write on Demand

**PROMPT** How do tornadoes affect the environment? Use details from the article to support your answer. Write for 5 minutes. Write as much as you can, as well as you can.

# The **Big** Question

**What makes a good story?**

**Theme Launcher Video**

 **LOG ON** ▶ Find out more about storytellers at www.macmillanmh.com.

Storytelling has always been popular. The oldest stories, such as myths, legends, and folktales, were usually passed on from person to person.

People can also share stories through writing, drawing, or acting. By sharing our stories, we share our history, our dreams, and our ideas. Hearing other people's stories helps us learn about the world around us.

## Research Activities

Throughout the unit, you will read different types of stories. Think of a classic story that you would like to research. Do research to find the tale's origin and learn more about how it has changed over time.

## Keep Track of Ideas

As you read, keep track of what you are learning about storytelling. Use the Layered Book to organize your ideas. On the front sheet, write the Unit Theme: Storytellers. On each layer, write what you learn about the different types of storytellers you read about each week.

**FOLDABLES®**
**Study Organizer**

Unit Theme
Week 1
Week 2
Week 3
Week 4
Week 5

# Research Toolkit

## Conduct Your Unit 6 Research Online with:

### Research Roadmap
Follow step-by-step guide to complete your research project.

### Online Resources
- Topic Finder and other Research Tools
- Videos and Virtual Fieldtrips
- Photos and Drawings for Presentations
- Related Articles and Web Resources

### California Web Site Links

 Go to **www.macmillanmh.com** for more information.

## California People

### Rudolfo Anaya, Hispanic American Storyteller
Rudolfo Anaya is from the American Southwest. He is one of the most widely read authors in Hispanic communities. His novels, short stories, plays, and poems entertain both children and adults.

# FOLKTALES

How do people around the world share stories that are important to them?

LOG ON ▶ Find out more about folktales at **www.macmillanmh.com**.

# Family Feast

**by Arthur Stam**

It was time for our end-of-year class party, and everyone was having trouble coming up with good ideas, including me.

"How about a carnival with games and cotton candy?" said Penny.

"I know!" said Megan. "A talent show with prizes and pizza!"

"Those are great ideas," said Mr. Ortiz. "What do you think about inviting our families to be **guests** at a foods-of-the-world festival? We can each bring our family's favorite dish. All of that food will make a lovely **banquet**."

The class liked the idea and seemed **agreeable** to it. I couldn't wait to see what dishes would arrive on the day of our party!

"My family loves Italian food," said Sophia on the morning of the party. "I brought spaghetti and meatballs."

"This is our favorite," said Sam. "It's lamb curry from India."

"Wait until you taste my Mexican tamales," said Elena.

I looked at all the strange dishes with great **curiosity**. Mr. Ortiz watched me **gaze** at each dish. He thought I was **untrusting**. "I can't wait to try some of these foods, Mr. Ortiz," I said.

I tried chicken stew from Kenya, German sausages, Greek salad, and more. All of it was delicious!

Not only did I eat a world of food, I met a world of families, too. We all did. What a day!

## Reread for **Comprehension**

### Visualize

**Make Inferences** When authors develop a plot, they do not always tell readers every detail. Sometimes readers have to **make inferences** to figure out missing information. To make inferences, use story clues and what you already know. You can also visualize, or picture, what is happening to help you make inferences. Reread the selection. Use your Inference Map to figure out details the author left out.

| Clue |
|------|
| Clue |
| Clue |
| Inference |

## Genre

A **Folktale** is a story based on the customs and traditions of a people or region; handed down orally from one generation to the next.

## Visualize

**Make Inferences**

As you read, use your Inference Map.

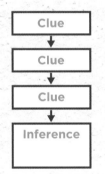

| Clue |
|:---:|

↓

| Clue |
|:---:|

↓

| Clue |
|:---:|

↓

| Inference |
|:---:|

## Read to Find Out

What do the people of the village learn from making stone soup?

# STONE SOUP

Award Winning Author

retold and
illustrated by
**Jon J Muth**

**THREE MONKS,** Hok, Lok, and Siew, traveled along a mountain road. They talked about cat whiskers, the color of the sun, and giving.

"What makes one happy, Siew?" asked Hok, the youngest monk.

Old Siew, who was the wisest, said, "Let's find out."

**Make Inferences**
What do you think makes the monks happy?

The sound of a bell brought their **gaze** to the rooftops of a village below. They could not see from so high above that the village had been through many hard times. Famine, floods, and war had made the villagers weary and **untrusting** of strangers. They had even become suspicious of their neighbors.

The villagers worked hard, but only for themselves.

There was a farmer.

A tea merchant.

A scholar.

A seamstress.

A doctor.

A carpenter ...

... and many others.

But they had little to do with one another.

When the monks reached the foot of the mountain, the villagers disappeared into their houses. No one came to the gates to greet them.

And when the people saw them enter the village, they closed their windows tight.

The monks knocked on the door of the first house. There was no answer. Then the house went dark.

They knocked on a second door and the same thing happened.

It happened again and again, from one house to the next.

"These people do not know happiness," they all agreed.

"But today," said Siew, his face bright as the moon, "we will show them how to make stone soup."

**Make Inferences**
Why do the monks think that the villagers are not happy?

They gathered twigs and branches and made a fire.

They placed a small tin pot on top and filled it with water from the village well.

A brave little girl who had been watching came to them. "What are you doing?" she asked.

"We are gathering twigs," said Lok.

"We are making a fire," said Hok.

"We are making stone soup and we need three round, smooth stones," said Siew.

The little girl helped the monks look around the courtyard until they found just the right ones. Then they put them in the water to cook.

"These stones will make excellent soup," said Siew. "But this very small pot won't make much I'm afraid."

"My mother has a bigger pot," said the girl.

The little girl ran home. As she started to take a pot, her mother asked what she was doing.

"The three strangers are making soup from stones," she said. "They need our biggest pot."

"Hmm," said the girl's mother. "Stones are easy to come by. I'd like to learn how to do that!"

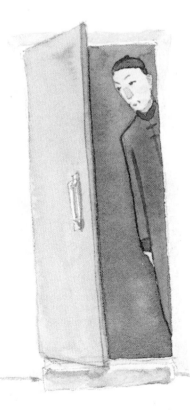

The monks poked the coals. As smoke drifted up, the neighbors peered out from their windows. The fire and the large pot in the middle of the village was a true **curiosity**!

One by one, the people of the village came out to see just what this stone soup was.

"Of course, old-style stone soup should be well seasoned with salt and pepper," said Hok.

"That is true," said Lok as he stirred the giant pot filled with water and stones. "But we have none ..."

"I have some salt and pepper!" said the scholar, his eyes big with curiosity. He disappeared and came back with salt and pepper and even a few other spices.

Siew took a taste. "The last time we had soup stones of this size and color, carrots made the broth very sweet."

"Carrots?" said a woman from the back. "I may have a few carrots! But just a few." And off she ran. She returned with as many carrots as she could carry and dropped them into the pot.

"Do you think it would be better with onions?" asked Hok.

"Oh, yes, maybe an onion would taste good," said a farmer, and he hurried off. He returned in a moment with five big onions, and he dropped them into the bubbling soup.

"Now, that's a fine soup!" he said.

The villagers all nodded their heads, as the smell was very **agreeable**.

"But if only we had some mushrooms," said Siew, rubbing his chin.

Several villagers licked their lips. A few dashed away and returned with fresh mushrooms, noodles, pea pods, and cabbages.

Something magical began to happen among the villagers. As each person opened their heart to give, the next person gave even more. And as this happened, the soup grew richer and smelled more delicious.

"I imagine the Emperor would suggest we add dumplings!" said one villager.

"And bean curd!" said another.

"What about cloud ear and mung beans and yams?" cried some others.

"And taro root and winter melon and baby corn!" cried other villagers.

"Garlic!" "Ginger Root!" "Soy sauce!" "Lily buds!"

"I have some! I have some!" people cried out. And off they ran, returning with all they could carry.

The monks stirred and the pot bubbled. How good it smelled! How good it would taste! How giving the villagers had become!

At last, the soup was ready. The villagers gathered together. They brought rice and steamed buns. They brought lychee nuts and sweet cakes. They brought tea to drink, and they lit lanterns.

Everyone sat down to eat. They had not been together for a feast like this for as long as anyone could remember.

After the **banquet**, they told stories, sang songs, and celebrated long into the night.

Then they unlocked their doors and took the monks into their homes and gave them very comfortable places to sleep.

In the gentle spring morning, everyone gathered together near the willows to say farewell.

"Thank you for having us as your **guests**," said the monks. "You have been most generous."

"Thank you," said the villagers. "With the gifts you have given, we will always have plenty. You have shown us that sharing makes us all richer."

"And to think," said the monks, "to be happy is as simple as making stone soup."

**Make Inferences**
How do the monks feel at the end of the story?

# The Soup on Jon J Muth

**Jon J Muth** can take old stories and turn them into new ones by setting them in different places. He took an old tale from Europe to write this Chinese story. When Jon was a boy, his mother took him to museums all across the United States. Later, he studied art in Asia and Europe. As Jon illustrates a book, he imagines that he is a boy running around inside the story. Then he can see things the way a child does.

**Other books** by Jon J Muth: *Come On, Rain!* and *The Three Questions*

LOG ON ▶ Find out more about Jon J Muth at **www.macmillanmh.com**.

**CA Author's Purpose**

What clues can help you figure out Jon J Muth's purpose for writing *Stone Soup*?

# CA Critical Thinking

## Summarize

Summarize what the monks did in *Stone Soup*. Use your Inference Map to help you explain why they wanted to make the soup.

| Clue |
|------|
| Clue |
| Clue |
| Inference |

## Think and Compare

1. What **inference** can you make about the monks' choice to stop at this village to make stone soup? Use details and information from the story to explain your answer. **Visualize: Make Inferences**

2. Look at pages 298–299. How have the villagers at the **banquet** changed from the beginning of the story? Use the illustrations and the text to support your answer. **Analyze**

3. If you were a villager in this story, would you have helped make stone soup? Why or why not? **Apply**

4. Explain how the world might change if more people shared. **Apply**

5. Read "Family Feast" on pages 280–281. Compare the class banquet with the village feast in *Stone Soup.* How are they alike? How are they different? Use details from both selections in your answer. **Reading/Writing Across Texts**

**Genre**

Nonfiction gives information about real people, places, or things.

**Text Feature**

Charts organize related information into categories.

**Content Vocabulary**

unique

tortillas

hearty

kimchi

chapatis

# What's for Lunch?

## by Leonard Mercury

What will you eat for lunch today? In some countries, lunchtime often means soup time! There are many kinds of **unique**, or different, soups served around the world. Some are as thin and clear as water. Some are as thick as stews. Others are full of noodles!

Soup is just one thing that can be eaten for lunch. What you eat for lunch may be different from the lunch of someone who lives in another country. Let's take a look around the world to see what kids are eating for lunch.

## Mexico: Tasting Tortillas

Many children in Mexico eat **tortillas** (tor·TEE·yas) for lunch. Most tortillas are made from ground corn, but sometimes wheat flour is used. Tortillas are usually flat and round. They are heated and filled with eggs, beans, or meat. Cheese and tasty sauces, called salsas, are often added. These sauces are made from chopped tomatoes, onions, hot peppers, and spices. Salsas add flavor and vitamins.

## Russia: Sipping Soup

Winters in Russia are very cold. Maybe that's why many Russian children eat soup for lunch. Two of their favorites are cabbage soup and beet soup.

Many Russian soups also include potatoes. Potatoes are an important crop in Russia. They make soups thick and **hearty**. Eating thick soups can help keep people warm and can fill them up so hunger is no problem!

## School Lunches Around the World

### Reading a Chart

Charts organize ideas into columns and rows.

This chart has two headings in the first row: "Country" and "School Lunches." Down the first column, you can read the country names. The second column shows what is eaten in each place.

| Country | School Lunches |
| --- | --- |
| Russia | beet or potato soup; wheat or rye bread |
| Mexico | tortillas with black beans and salsa |
| India | chapatis with dal |
| Thailand | rice noodles with tofu, shrimp, and peanuts |
| South Korea | squid with hot sauce, rice, radish kimchi |

## South Korea: Passing the Pickles

Meals in Korea are made up of many dishes. No matter what else is served, there is always rice.

**Kimchi** (KIM·chee) is also always on the table. Kimchi is pickled meat or vegetables. Korean children mix together many dishes and flavors at meals. It's common for their food to be hot and spicy.

## Thailand: Eating Noodles at Noon

Lunch in Thailand often includes noodles. There are many ways to serve noodles. One popular dish is made with thin rice noodles, tofu, and shrimp. Another favorite way to eat rice noodles is with meat, vegetables, and thick gravy.

## India: Chewing on Chapatis

Many children living in India eat **chapatis** (chuh·PAH·tees) for lunch. Chapatis are made from only two ingredients: wheat flour and water. The flour and water are mixed into dough. The dough is rolled flat and thin. It's cooked on a hot griddle until it puffs up. Then it's held over an open flame.

Some children like dal (dahl) with their chapatis. Dal looks like a very thick soup. It is spicy and delicious!

##  Critical Thinking

1. Look at the chart on page 305. What kind of soups do children eat for school lunch in Russia? **Reading a Chart**

2. Based on what you know, where in the world would you like to eat lunch? Explain your answer. **Evaluate**

3. Think about this article and *Stone Soup.* What ingredients might people from Russia, Mexico, India, Thailand, and South Korea have brought to put in the soup? **Reading/ Writing Across Texts**

 ### History/Social Science Activity

Learn what kids eat for lunch in a country not on the chart, such as Australia, Iran, or Greece. Copy the chart and add your new row of information to it.

 Find out more about lunch at www.macmillanmh.com.

✔ **Believable Characters**

Good writers give their characters realistic actions and realistic dialogue to make them believable to the reader.

# Reading and Writing Connection

Read the passage below. Notice how the author creates believable conversation between mother and daughter.

**An excerpt from**
*Stone Soup*

The author shows how a real mother and daughter might act. We start to believe that the mother became interested in making stone soup.

The little girl ran home. As she started to take a pot, her mother asked what she was doing.

"The three strangers are making soup from stones," she said. "They need our biggest pot."

"Hmm," said the girl's mother. "Stones are easy to come by. I'd like to learn how to do that!"

STONE SOUP

retold and illustrated by
Jon J Muth

# Read and Find

Read Grace's writing below. How did she help us learn about the character of Sarah? Use the Writer's Checklist to help you.

## Sarah's Morning

### By Grace F.

"Oops!" Sarah said while grabbing a sponge from the sink. She wiped so it was good enough for her, but not for most people. You could still see orange puddles of juice. Sarah turned to Spot, her favorite pet, and waved good-bye. She threw on her coat as she raced toward the front door. She heard the bus just pulling up.

Read my story about Sarah's morning.

## Writer's Checklist

✓ Does it make sense that Sarah would wave to her dog before leaving?

✓ What question could you ask Sarah about herself?

☑ Can you figure out at least one thing that is important to Sarah?

## Talk About It

Plays tell a story. How do costumes make plays more fun to watch?

**LOG ON** ▶ Find out more about plays at **www.macmillanmh.com**.

# PLAYS

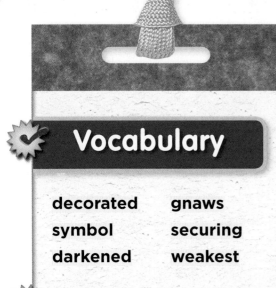
# The Wind and the Sun

## an Aesop's Fable

*retold by Jon Lory*

**NARRATOR:** Long ago, Wind and Sun argued about which of them was stronger. In the middle of the argument, they saw a man walking down the road. He wore a coat that was **decorated** with a picture of a gold ax on the front. The ax was the **symbol** of his trade. He was a woodcutter.

**SUN:** Let's try to get that coat off the woodcutter. Whoever can do that is stronger. You go first.

**NARRATOR:** Wind went first. Sun hid behind a cloud to watch from the **darkened** sky.

**WIND:** I will blow on the woodcutter as hard as I can. I know I can blow off that coat!

**NARRATOR:** So Wind blew on the woodcutter as hard as he could.

**WIND:** Whoooosh … whoooosh-whoooosh … WHOOOOOSH!

**WOODCUTTER:** Oh! How the cold wind **gnaws** at my bones. It is good that I have this warm coat to wrap around me.

**NARRATOR:** The woodcutter walked on, **securing** his coat even tighter around him. Wind gave up in despair.

**WIND:** That must have been the **weakest** wind I have ever made! It could not blow the coat off the woodcutter.

**NARRATOR:** It was now Sun's turn to try.

**SUN:** I will shine my rays on the woodcutter as hard as I can. I know that I will be able to remove that coat!

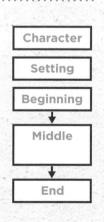

**NARRATOR:** So Sun shined on the woodcutter as hard as he could.

**WOODCUTTER:** Oh! How hot the sun shines. It is far too warm for this coat! It is good that I can take it off.

**NARRATOR:** So the woodcutter took off his coat, which proved that Sun was indeed stronger than Wind.

---

## Reread for **Comprehension**

### Generate Questions

**Summarize** Generating, or asking, questions as you read can help you **summarize** a story. Ask yourself what happens at the beginning, middle, and end. A Story Map can help you keep track of characters, setting, and events in a story. You can then use what you have learned to summarize the story.

Reread the selection. Then use your Story Map to summarize the story.

| Character |
| --- |
| Setting |
| Beginning |
| ↓ |
| Middle |
| ↓ |
| End |

## CA Comprehension

### Genre

A **Play** is a story that is performed before an audience.

### Generate Questions

**Summarize**

As you read, use your Story Map.

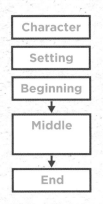

Character

↓

Setting

↓

Beginning

↓

Middle

↓

End

### Read to Find Out

How does Little Red Ant find out who is the strongest one?

314

# The Strongest One

## A Zuni Play

By Joseph Bruchac

Illustrated by Lucia Angela Perez

Award Winning Author

THE ZUNIS are one of the people of the Southwest who dwell in pueblos, compact villages made up of multistoried buildings of adobe brick and beams. The Zunis' pueblo, which is also called Zuni, is located in present-day New Mexico. The Zunis and the other pueblo people developed means of growing their crops in the dry lands of the Southwest and are regarded as very sophisticated farmers.

The Zuni people are famous for their ceremonies, which are designed to give thanks and support to all living things, from the largest to the smallest. The Zunis are also very well known as artists for their beautiful jewelry made of silver and turquoise.

# CHARACTERS

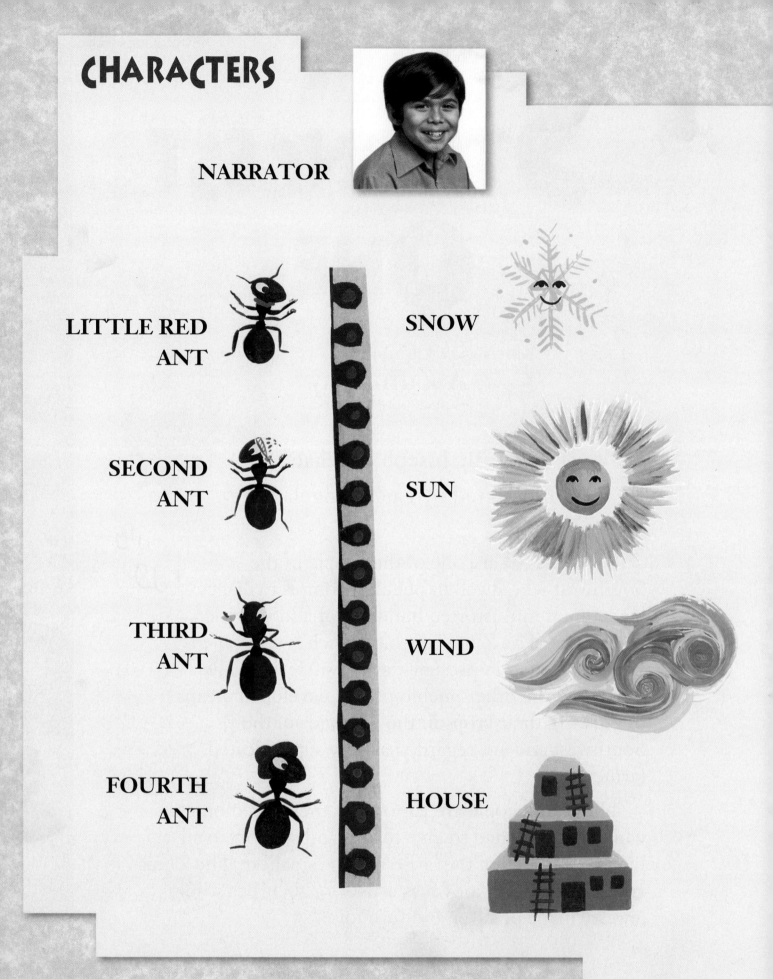

NARRATOR

LITTLE RED ANT

SECOND ANT

THIRD ANT

FOURTH ANT

SNOW

SUN

WIND

HOUSE

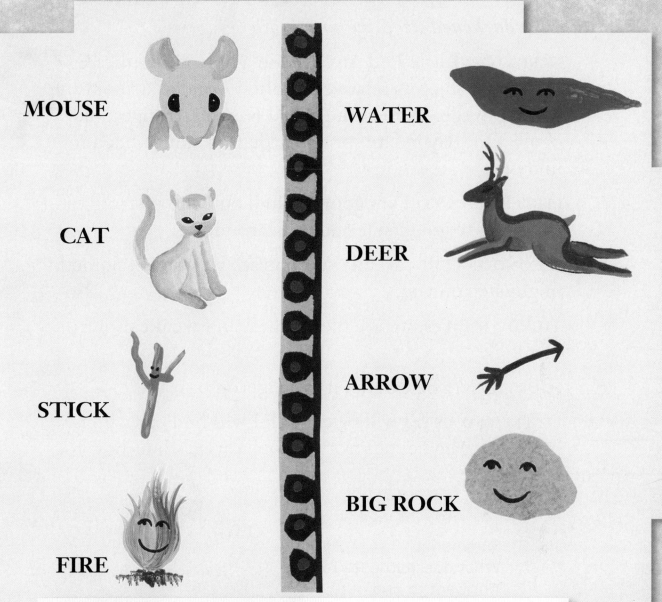

MOUSE

CAT

STICK

FIRE

WATER

DEER

ARROW

BIG ROCK

## COSTUMES

NARRATOR wears long head scarf tied at the side.

THE ANTS wear feelers suggested by **securing** red pipe cleaners around a headband.

SNOW, SUN, WIND, STICK, FIRE, WATER, BIG ROCK all wear t-shirts **decorated** with their **symbol**.

HOUSE carries a large paper cutout depicting an adobe.

MOUSE, CAT, DEER can be suggested with felt tails, and felt ears secured to a headband.

ARROW carries a large cardboard arrow.

## Scene 1: Inside the Ants' Hole

*On a **darkened** stage, the ants crouch together.*

**NARRATOR:** Little Red Ant lived in a hole under the Big Rock with all of its relatives. It often wondered about the world outside: Who in the world was the strongest one of all? One day in late spring Little Red Ant decided to find out.

**LITTLE RED ANT:** I am going to find out who is strongest. I am going to go outside and walk around.

**SECOND ANT:** Be careful! We ants are very small. Something might step on you.

**THIRD ANT:** Yes, we are the smallest and **weakest** ones of all.

**FOURTH ANT:** Be careful, it is dangerous out there!

**LITTLE RED ANT:** I will be careful. I will find out who is strongest. Maybe the strongest one can teach us how to be stronger.

**Summarize**
What does Little Red Ant want to find out?

## SCENE II: THE MESA

*Ant walks back and forth onstage.*

**NARRATOR:** So Little Red Ant went outside and began to walk around. But as Little Red Ant walked, the snow began to fall.

*Snow walks onstage.*

**LITTLE RED ANT:** Ah, my feet are cold. This snow makes everything freeze. Snow must be the strongest. I will ask. Snow, are you the strongest of all?

**SNOW:** No, I am not the strongest.

**LITTLE RED ANT:** Who is stronger than you?

**SNOW:** Sun is stronger. When Sun shines on me, I melt away. Here it comes!

*As Sun walks onstage, Snow hurries offstage.*

**LITTLE RED ANT:** Ah, Sun must be the strongest. I will ask. Sun, are you the strongest of all?

**SUN:** No, I am not the strongest.

**LITTLE RED ANT:** Who is stronger than you?

**SUN:** Wind is stronger. Wind blows the clouds across the sky and covers my face. Here it comes!

*As Wind comes onstage, Sun hurries offstage with face covered in hands.*

**LITTLE RED ANT:** Wind must be the strongest. I will ask. Wind, are you the strongest of all?

**WIND:** No, I am not the strongest.

**LITTLE RED ANT:** Who is stronger than you?

**WIND:** House is stronger. When I come to House, I cannot move it. I must go elsewhere. Here it comes!

*As House walks onstage, Wind hurries offstage.*

**LITTLE RED ANT:** House must be the strongest. I will ask. House, are you the strongest of all?

**HOUSE:** No, I am not the strongest.

**LITTLE RED ANT:** Who is stronger than you?

**HOUSE:** Mouse is stronger. Mouse comes and **gnaws** holes in me. Here it comes!

*As Mouse walks onstage, House hurries offstage.*

**LITTLE RED ANT:** Mouse must be the strongest. I will ask. Mouse, are you the strongest of all?

**MOUSE:** No, I am not the strongest.

**LITTLE RED ANT:** Who is stronger than you?

**MOUSE:** Cat is stronger. Cat chases me, and if Cat catches me, Cat will eat me. Here it comes!

*As Cat walks onstage, Mouse hurries offstage, squeaking.*

**LITTLE RED ANT:** Cat must be the strongest. I will ask. Cat, are you the strongest of all?

**CAT:** No, I am not the strongest.

**LITTLE RED ANT:** Who is stronger than you?

**CAT:** Stick is stronger. When Stick hits me, I run away. Here it comes!

*As Stick walks onstage, Cat hurries offstage, meowing.*

**LITTLE RED ANT:** Stick must be the strongest. I will ask. Stick, are you the strongest of all?

**STICK:** No, I am not the strongest.

**LITTLE RED ANT:** Who is stronger than you?

**STICK:** Fire is stronger. When I am put into Fire, Fire burns me up! Here it comes!

*As Fire walks onstage, Stick hurries offstage.*

**LITTLE RED ANT:** Fire must be the strongest. I will ask. Fire, are you the strongest of all?

**FIRE:** No, I am not the strongest.

**LITTLE RED ANT:** Who is stronger than you?

**FIRE:** Water is stronger. When Water is poured on me, it kills me. Here it comes!

*As Water walks onstage, Fire hurries offstage.*

**LITTLE RED ANT:** Water must be the strongest. I will ask. Water, are you the strongest of all?

**WATER:** No, I am not the strongest.

**LITTLE RED ANT:** Who is stronger than you?

**WATER:** Deer is stronger. When Deer comes, Deer drinks me. Here it comes!

*As Deer walks onstage, Water hurries offstage.*

**LITTLE RED ANT:** Deer must be the strongest. I will ask. Deer, are you the strongest of all?

**DEER:** No, I am not the strongest.

**LITTLE RED ANT:** Who is stronger than you?

**DEER:** Arrow is stronger. When Arrow strikes me, it can kill me. Here it comes!

*As Arrow walks onstage, Deer runs offstage with leaping bounds.*

**LITTLE RED ANT:** Arrow must be the strongest. I will ask. Arrow, are you the strongest of all?

**ARROW:** No, I am not the strongest.

**LITTLE RED ANT:** Who is stronger than you?

**ARROW:** Big Rock is stronger. When I am shot from the bow and I hit Big Rock, Big Rock breaks me.

**LITTLE RED ANT:** Do you mean the same Big Rock where the Red Ants live?

**ARROW:** Yes, that is Big Rock. Here it comes!

*As Big Rock walks onstage, Arrow runs offstage.*

**LITTLE RED ANT:** Big Rock must be the strongest. I will ask. Big Rock, are you the strongest of all?

**BIG ROCK:** No, I am not the strongest.

**LITTLE RED ANT:** Who is stronger than you?

**BIG ROCK:** You are stronger. Every day you and the other Red Ants come and carry little pieces of me away. Someday I will be all gone.

## Scene III: The Ants' Hole

**NARRATOR:** So Little Red Ant went back home and spoke to the ant people.

*The ants crouch together on the darkened stage.*

**SECOND ANT:** Little Red Ant has returned.

**THIRD ANT:** He has come back alive!

**FOURTH ANT:** Tell us about what you have learned. Who is the strongest of all?

**LITTLE RED ANT:** I have learned that everything is stronger than something else. And even though we ants are small, in some ways *we* are the strongest of all.

> **Summarize**
> What has Little Red Ant discovered about who is strongest?

# WHO'S STRONGER THAN JOE AND LUCIA?

## AUTHOR

JOSEPH BRUCHAC was raised in the Adirondack Mountains by his Native American grandparents. As a child, Joseph wanted to share stories about his heritage. When he grew up, he began to write the traditional tales of his people. One day when Joseph was reading one of his books to an audience, he began to tell the tale from memory, just as Native American storytellers did a long time ago. Now Joseph writes and tells his tales.

**Other books** by Joseph Bruchac: *The Earth Under Sky Bear's Feet* and *The First Strawberries*

## ILLUSTRATOR

LUCIA ANGELA PEREZ was introduced to art at an early age. Her mother was a painter and had a pottery business. Lucia became a book illustrator when she finished a book that her mother began. Lucia has been working as an illustrator ever since. She now lives with her family in Texas.

**LOG ON** ▶ Find out more about Joseph Bruchac and Lucia Angela Perez at **www.macmillanmh.com**.

**CA Author's Purpose**

Why did Joseph Bruchac write *The Strongest One*? Find three details that give clues to the author's purpose.

 **Critical Thinking**

## Summarize

Use your Story Map to help you summarize *The Strongest One*. Tell about the characters, setting, and events in the beginning, middle, and end of the story.

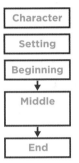

| Character |
| Setting |
| Beginning |
| Middle |
| End |

## Think and Compare

1.  What details about the characters and setting does the author include in Scene I that help you **summarize** the play? **Generate Questions: Summarize**

2.  Think about what each character tells Little Red Ant. Use story details to explain how the characters are strong and weak at the same time. **Synthesize**

3.  Think of something that is bigger than you. Tell why it is stronger or weaker. **Apply**

4.  Little Red Ant learns a lesson about being the strongest. Why is this an important lesson for people to learn? Explain. **Evaluate**

5.  Compare the Wind from "The Wind and the Sun" on pages 312–313 with the ants in *The Strongest One*. Where in the stories do the characters feel the **weakest**? What do they learn about being strong? **Reading/Writing Across Texts**

# THE Big Dipper

By Guadalupe V. Lopez

On a clear, dark night you can look up and see stars twinkle brightly. Have you noticed that some are brighter than others and they are clustered in groups?

Thousands of years ago, people studied the stars and created tales about them. They imagined that groups of stars formed shapes. They imagined animals, objects, and people. These star patterns are called **constellations**. One of the most famous star patterns is the **Big Dipper**.

# Follow the Stars

Long ago, people used a **dipper** to get water. A dipper has a long handle and a cup. The Big Dipper is named for this shape. The Big Dipper is an important constellation because of its position in the sky.

The two stars that form the front of the Big Dipper's cup are called "pointer stars." They point the way to the **North Star**. Ship captains of long ago used the Big Dipper as a **compass** to help them find their way.

# Find the North Star

## Reading a Diagram

This diagram helps you see the shape of the Big Dipper. On a clear night, see if you can locate it. Follow the pointer stars to the North Star.

North Star

Big Dipper

# Compass in the Sky

The Big Dipper has been a compass but it has also been used as a calendar in the sky. The Big Dipper rotates around the North Star through the seasons. Read how the Big Dipper can help you know the seasons.

**In Summer, the Big Dipper is to the left of the North Star. The handle sticks up, like a stalk of corn swaying in the summer breeze.**

**In Spring, the Big Dipper is above the North Star. It looks like a dipper dropping seeds on the soil.**

Spring

Summer

North Star

Fall

Winter

**In the Fall, the cup of the Big Dipper is open to the sky. It looks like a wheelbarrow. Can you imagine it full of corn after the harvest?**

**In Winter, the Big Dipper is to the right of the North Star. The handle hangs down like an icicle.**

# An Iroquois Legend

*Long ago, many cultures made up stories
to explain why groups of stars seem to move
across the night sky from season to season.*

Long ago and far away, a group of Iroquois hunters were chasing a bear through the woods. Suddenly, the Iroquois came upon three giants. The giants attacked the Iroquois. Only three of the hunters survived. The three Iroquois and the bear were transported up to the sky. There, the chase continues to this day in the Big Dipper. The three stars in the handle of the dipper represent the three Iroquois hunters. The four stars in the cup of the dipper are the bear.

## CA Critical Thinking

1. Look at the diagram. Find the stars that help you find the North Star. Describe how they help you find the North Star. **Reading a Diagram**

2. How do you think the Big Dipper helped people of long ago when they wanted to know about the seasons? **Analyze**

3. Compare "An Iroquois Legend" and *The Strongest One*. How are the Iroquois hunters like the characters in *The Strongest One*? Support your answer with details from the selections. **Reading/Writing Across Texts**

### Science Activity

Research another constellation. Draw a diagram of this constellation in the night sky. Label any major stars.

LOG ON ▶ Find out more at
www.macmillanmh.com.

# Reading and Writing Connection

## Believable Characters

Good writers make characters believable through their thoughts, dialogue, and actions.

Read the passage below. Notice how author Joseph Bruchac creates one ant who seems to think for himself.

**An excerpt from**
*The Strongest One*

The author numbers all of the ants except for the Little Red Ant. That ant seems to have something to say that everyone wants to listen to.

Narrator: So Little Red Ant went back home and spoke to the ant people.

Second Ant: Little Red Ant has returned.

Third Ant: He has come back alive!

Fourth Ant: Tell us what you have learned. Who is the strongest of all?

Little Red Ant: I have learned that everything is stronger than something else. And even though we ants are small, in some ways *we* are the strongest of all.

THE STRONGEST ONE

A Zuni Play

By Joseph Bruchac
Illustrated by Lucia Angel Perez

## Read and Find

Read Kaylicia's writing below. How did she make Rose Alia into a believable character? Use the Writer's Checklist to help you.

# Rose Alia's Birthday

### By Kaylicia M.

Rose Alia found the box underneath the bed and unwrapped it. It really was the play oven she wanted! Rose Alia had a big imagination. She imagined that if she had a play oven, she could cook like the people on TV. She imagined walking on a big stage in a chef's uniform and hat. She always wanted to wear that hat!

Read my story about Rose Alia's birthday gift.

---

# Writer's Checklist

✔ Does Kaylicia show you that something really matters to Rose Alia?

✔ Do you know enough about Rose Alia's imagination to know why she wants a play oven?

☑ Can you imagine asking Rose Alia a question?

335

What are the different ways people tell stories? What can stories teach us?

 Find out more about storytelling at **www.macmillanmh.com**.

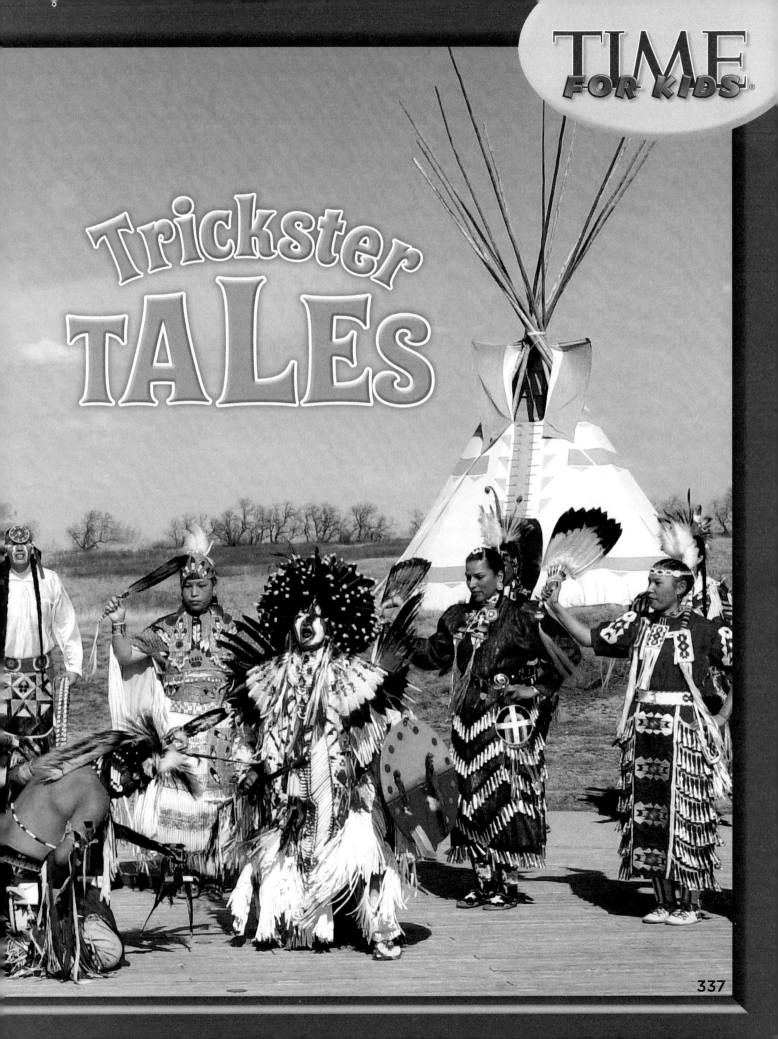

# Trickster TALES

## Vocabulary

- insightful
- technique
- investigate
- cunning
- majority

**Children enjoy the stories at Jonesboro.**

# Telling Tales

Do you like to hear stories? Then Jonesboro, Tennessee, is the place for you. That's where the National Storytelling Festival has been held each year since 1973. The festival's founders wanted people to enjoy the art of storytelling. Today, more than 10,000 visitors laugh and cry as they listen to **insightful** storytellers.

Why is storytelling so popular? Stories tell us about our past—and maybe about our future. "Long ago, when there were no books or TV, it was the storyteller's job to explain why there are stars in the sky, why we laugh and cry," says California storyteller Brenda Wong Aoki.

"Everyone can be a good storyteller. That's what we do every day," says Syd Lieberman, a storyteller from Chicago. One **technique** for telling stories is to describe your everyday life. Says Lieberman, "When you say, 'Mom, listen to what happened today,' that's the beginning of a story."

# TOP 5 FAVORITE KIDS' BOOKS

What's the best book you have ever read? Here are some favorites. Maybe you'd like to **investigate** the work of some of these writers.

| Book Title | Author | Date first published |
|---|---|---|
| **1.** Harry Potter (series) | J.K. Rowling | 1997 |
| **2.** Goosebumps *(series)* | R.L. Stine | 1992 |
| **3.** *Green Eggs and Ham* | Dr. Seuss | 1960 |
| **4.** *The Cat in the Hat* | Dr. Seuss | 1957 |
| **5.** Arthur (series) | Marc Brown | 1976 |

Survey based on 1,800 students aged 7–15. Source: National Education Association

# Super Storytellers

If there were a storyteller hall of fame, these clever and **cunning** people would be in it. Listen up!

**Homer**  The ancient Greeks told stories about gods and heroes. A blind poet named Homer retold these myths. His famous books are the *Illiad* and the *Odyssey*.

**Aesop**  Also in ancient Greece, a man named Aesop made up fantastic fables with animal characters. Fables like the "Tortoise and the Hare" teach a moral or lesson.

**Hans Christian Andersen**  In the 1800s, Hans Christian Andersen told such stories as "The Princess and the Pea" and "The Ugly Duckling" to children in many towns. The **majority** of his stories came from folktales.

**CA Comprehension**

### Genre

**Nonfiction** Some nonfiction articles give information about real people, places, and things.

### Generate Questions

**Compare and Contrast**
When authors compare two topics or ideas, they often use signal words, such as *similar* and *different*.

# Tales of the Trickster

**How do storytellers explain the world we live in?**

Where does the wind come from? Why is there night? Why does a leopard have spots? Nowadays, scientists **investigate** and answer questions like these. But long ago, people made up stories to explain how the world works. Some of these stories were trickster tales.

## Meet the Trickster

A trickster is a character in a story. Tricksters use their wits to get what they want. Sometimes they trick other characters. Sometimes they are the ones being tricked. A trickster doesn't always have the same name or even the same body. He is often an animal with human features, such as a coyote, fox, tortoise, or spider.

## The Trickster Animals

Like an actor playing different parts in different movies, the trickster has many roles. For example, the trickster character varies in Native American stories. He can be a **cunning** coyote in a story from the Crow nation. He may be a brave raven in a story from the Pacific Northwest. Or the trickster may be a spider dressed in deerskin clothes in a Dakota Territory tale.

## The Way Things Work

Native American trickster tales were spoken, not written. They were passed down from one storyteller to the next. However, each person puts his or her own stamp on the story.

Oral stories are different from written stories. Written stories stay the same on a page. They may pass from generation to generation this way. Spoken stories are different because they can change over time. A storyteller doesn't always memorize a tale word for word. The storyteller might remember important parts at the beginning, middle, and end. As a result, no two stories are ever told exactly the same.

Storyteller Robert Greygrass has Lakota and Cherokee roots.

## Native American Storytellers

Robert Greygrass is a Native American storyteller who was born in California. He has appeared in many storytelling events, such as the Bay Area Storytelling Festival in El Sobrante, California. "He was great," said 10-year-old Patrick Whamond. "He told stories about animals and how things got to be the way they are."

Like other storytellers, Greygrass uses **insightful** tales to teach, inspire, and entertain. He tells many stories about the history of Native Americans. Some of his tales also describe mankind's place in the universe.

Another Native American storyteller is Rose Red Elk, or Red Feather Woman. She was born on a reservation in Poplar, Montana. When Rose was a child, her father and grandfather told her stories about her ancestors. Now a successful storyteller herself, she says, "Stories were used as teaching tools, lessons to learn in life, and history of the people."

The **majority** of Rose's tales are from Sioux and Assiniboine tribes. Unlike some other storytellers, Rose sets her words to music. She uses this **technique** to make her stories even more entertaining.

## Worldwide Tricksters

It isn't only Native Americans who tell trickster tales. Many countries have their own trickster stories. Korea's trickster shows up in "The Ungrateful Tiger," and children in India hear about "The Fish That Were Too Clever."

The trickster has a strong place in American folk traditions. Riccardo Salmona, who worked at the American Folk Art Museum in New York City says, "Trickster stories can pass along jokes, relay instructions on honoring the dead, preserve figures of speech—many things." Salmona adds, "They have become part of the fabric of our communities."

Rose Red Elk

**CA Critical Thinking**

1. Compare Rose Red Elk's storytelling with Robert Greygrass's storytelling. How are they alike? How are they different?

2. Name three animals that are trickster characters in stories.

3. Why do you think many people enjoy hearing stories more than reading them?

4. Do you think Robert Greygrass would agree with Brenda Wong Aoki's quote in "Telling Tales"? Why or why not?

343

CA Show What You Know

**Think and Search**

The answer is in more than one place. Keep reading to find the answer.

# Voices of the Past

At the end of the United States Civil War, about four million enslaved Africans were freed. Between 1932 and 1975, some recorded their stories. Twenty-three of these stories are now available for us to hear.

The recordings appear on the Library of Congress Web site. Here you can find storytellers who talk about their experiences. Many speak about the work they did, their families, and how they felt. Others tell about their later lives as free men and women.

Isom Moseley was a boy when he was freed. He remembers that things were slow to change. "It was a year before the folks knowed they was free," he says.

Michael Taft is the head of the library's archive of folk culture. He says the recordings let us know things that written stories can't. "It's how something is said that helps tell the story," Taft says.

A researcher interviewed Isom Moseley in 1941. ▲

Go on ▶

**Directions: Now answer Numbers 1–5. Base your answers on the article "Voices of the Past."**

1. The stories of the former slaves were recorded

    A    at the end of the Civil War.
    B    about 100 years ago.
    C    over 30 years ago.
    D    only 20 years ago.

2. Anyone can listen to some of these former slaves' stories by

    A    checking out DVDs at a local library.
    B    visiting the Library of Congress Web site.
    C    asking the people to tell their stories again.
    D    tuning in to the Library of Congress radio station.

3. Researchers recorded the stories of former slaves to

    A    prove that written stories are much better.
    B    sell on the Library of Congress Web site.
    C    show that most former slaves wouldn't talk about slavery.
    D    preserve the experiences of these people.

4. Why is it important to keep these old recordings instead of only keeping written documents? Use details from the article in your answer.

5. An author is writing a nonfiction book about the time before, during, and after the U.S. Civil War. Would this author be interested in listening to these interviews with former slaves? Why or why not?

**Tip**

Keep reading. The answer is in more than one place.

# ✏️ Write on Demand

**CA** Many people help animals and the environment.

Think about how you could help animals and the environment.

Now write to <u>explain how</u> you could help.

Expository writing explains, defines, or tells how to do something.

To figure out if a writing prompt asks for expository writing, look for clue words, such as <u>explain how</u> or <u>tell how</u>.

Below see how one student begins a response to the prompt above.

The writer included relevant facts and details that tell about the main idea.

> The Nature Preserve is a place that works to keep our town safe and clean for the birds and animals.
>
> Every weekend, the preserve shows kids how to do things that help. One thing you can do is build birdhouses. There are many birds in my town. People cut down trees to build new houses. Making birdhouses will help the bird population. The Nature Preserve has a room that shows the names of trees and plants that grow in my town. Our town is a special place and we should help to keep it that way!

# Writing Prompt

Respond in writing to the prompt below. Write for

15 minutes. Write as much as you can, as well as you can.

Review the hints below before and after you write.

> Everyone has an issue they feel strongly about.
>
> Think about something you care about.
>
> Now write a letter to persuade others to feel the same way.

## Writing Hints for Prompts

- ☑ Read the prompt carefully.
- ☑ Plan your writing by organizing your ideas.
- ☑ Support your ideas by telling more about each reason.
- ☑ Use a variety of sentence structures.
- ☑ Choose words that help others understand what you mean.
- ☑ Review and edit your writing.

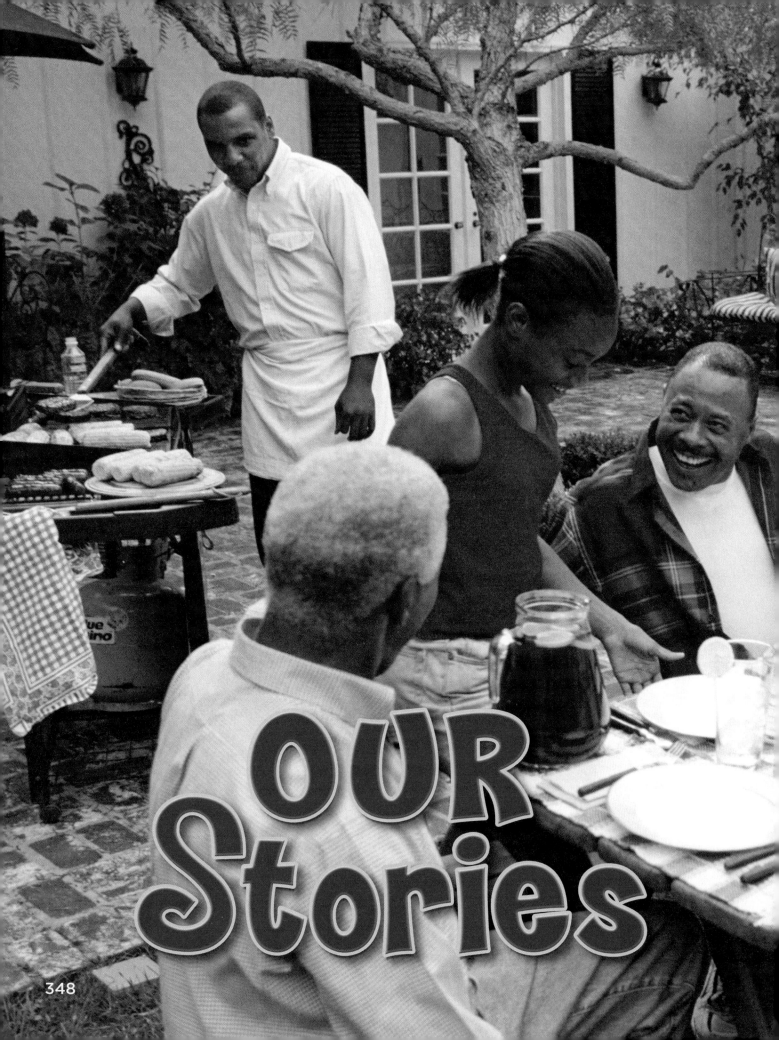

OUR Stories

## CA Talk About It

What kinds of stories do the members of your family share with one another?

**LOG ON** ▶ Find out more about stories from different cultures at **www.macmillanmh.com**.

# Red and Her Friends

*by Marilyn MacGregor*

A hen named Red lived in a city. Red and her pals did everything together. On Monday morning, as was their **tradition**, Red and her feline friend Fiona went shopping. As they passed a trash-filled, weed-covered lot, Red smiled. "Wouldn't that lot be a **magnificent** spot for a garden?" she asked.

Fiona didn't see eye to eye with Red. "This place is a mess. It's a disaster!"

"We'd have to clean it up, of course," said Red. She saw their friend Ricardo and asked him for help.

"Sorry. I have a dentist appointment," Ricardo barked and walked away wagging his tail.

Red was disappointed. Fiona hissed angrily.

"I'll help you," said Fiona.

Red and Fiona cleaned the lot. Then it was time to plant seeds.

"I wish I could help," said Ricardo as he passed by, "but I have bones to dig up."

"I'll help," said Fiona, shaking her head at the dog.

Red and Fiona planted carrots, pumpkins, and squash. Soon the seeds grew and made the garden beautiful. It looked like a **masterpiece**! Red asked her friends to help weed and water. Only Fiona had time to help. When it was time to pick the vegetables, only Red and Fiona did the work.

"I'll make dinner," said Red. "Each vegetable will be an **ingredient** in my **recipes** for cooking vegetable stew and pumpkin pie." Red licked her lips. "Those are **tasty** dishes."

Ricardo happened to walk by just then.

"I'd be happy to come to dinner," he said.

"You didn't help clean, weed, water, or pick. What makes you think you're invited?" asked Fiona. Red nodded firmly.

Of course, Fiona was invited, and everything was delicious.

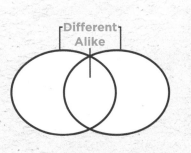

## Reread for **Comprehension**

### Make Inferences and Analyze

**Compare and Contrast** To **compare** and **contrast** is to tell how things are alike and different. To compare and contrast characters you need to make inferences about how the characters are alike and different.

A Venn diagram can help you compare characters.

Reread the selection to compare Fiona with Ricardo. As you read, think about each character's actions, traits, and feelings.

Different
Alike

## CA Comprehension

### Genre

**Fantasy** tells a story about invented characters who could not exist in real life.

### Make Inferences and Analyze

✔ **Compare and Contrast**
As you read, use your Venn diagram.

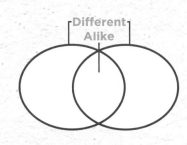

### Read to Find Out

Who will help Rooster bake a strawberry shortcake?

# Cook-a-Doodle-Doo!

by Janet Stevens and
Susan Stevens Crummel
illustrated by Janet Stevens

Award Winning Selection

Peck. Peck. Peck.

"Always chicken feed! Day after day—year after year—I'm sick of it!" squawked Big Brown Rooster. "Can we get something new to eat around here? Please? Nobody's listening. What's a hungry rooster to do?"

"There's no hope. Wait a minute …" Rooster remembered a story his mama used to tell, a story handed down from chicken to chicken. The story of his famous great-grandmother, the Little Red Hen.

Rooster rushed into the chicken coop. "It has to be here," he said. He looked high and low, and there it was at last, hidden under a nest—her cookbook. *The Joy of Cooking Alone* by L. R. Hen.

Rooster carefully turned the pages. "So many **recipes**—and I thought she just baked bread! Look at the strawberry shortcake!"

"That's it! I'll make the most wonderful, **magnificent** strawberry shortcake in the whole wide world. No more chicken feed for me!"

"Yes sirree—just like Great-Granny, I'll be a cook! COOK-A-DOODLE-DO-O-O!" crowed Rooster as he pranced toward the big farmhouse.

Compare and Contrast
How is Rooster like Great-Granny?
How is he different?

"*Cook*-a-doodle-doo?" said Dog.

"Have you lost your marbles, Rooster?" asked Cat.

"You've never cooked anything before!" said Goose.

"That doesn't matter," replied Rooster. "Cooking is in my blood—it's a family **tradition**. Now, who will help me?"

"Not I," said Dog.

"Not I," said Cat.

"Not I," said Goose.

And away they went.

Rooster pushed open the kitchen door. "It looks like I'm on my own … just like Great-Granny." He sighed and put on his apron.

"We'll help you."

Rooster turned, and there stood Turtle, Iguana, and Potbellied Pig.

"Do you three know anything about cooking?" Rooster asked.

"I can read recipes!" said Turtle.

"I can get stuff!" said Iguana.

"I can taste!" said Pig. "I'm an expert at tasting."

"Then we're a team," declared Rooster. "Let's get ready and start cooking!"

Turtle read the cookbook. "Heat oven to 450 degrees."

"I can do that!" said Iguana. "Look, I'll turn the knob. 150, 250, 350, 450. Hey, cooking is easy!"

Rooster put a big bowl on the table. "What's our first **ingredient**?" he asked.

"The recipe says we need flour," said Turtle.

"I can do that!" said Iguana. He dashed outside and picked a petunia. "How's this flower?"

# Little Red Hen's Magnificent Strawberry Shortcake

A cookbook gives directions for making many different things to eat. Each type of food has its own recipe—a list of everything that goes into it and step-by-step directions on how to make it.

One of the oven knobs controls the temperature of the oven. The higher the number on the knob, the hotter the oven. Temperature is measured in degrees Fahrenheit (°F) or degrees Celsius (°C). On a very hot day the temperature outside can be over 100°F (38°C). Can you imagine what 450°F (232°C) feels like?

Ingredients are the different things that go into a recipe. Each ingredient may not taste good by itself, but if you put them all together in the right way, the result tastes delicious.

"No, no, no," said Rooster. "Not *that* kind of flower. We need flour for *cooking*. You know, the fluffy white stuff that's made from wheat."

"Can I taste the flour?" asked Pig.

"Not yet, Pig," said Turtle. "The recipe says to sift it first."

"What does *sift* mean?" asked Iguana.

"Hmmm," said Turtle. "I think *sift* means 'to search through' ..."

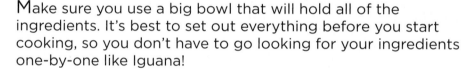

Make sure you use a big bowl that will hold all of the ingredients. It's best to set out everything before you start cooking, so you don't have to go looking for your ingredients one-by-one like Iguana!

Flour is made from wheat grains that are finely ground. Long ago, the grinding was done by hand; now it is done by machines. Rooster's Great-Granny had to grind the grain into flour by hand, but you and Rooster can buy flour at the grocery store.

You will find many different kinds of flour at the store—including all-purpose flour, whole-wheat flour, cake flour, and high-altitude flour. Rooster's recipe calls for all-purpose flour.

Sifting adds air to the flour so it can be measured accurately. Some sifters have cranks, some have spring-action handles, and some are battery powered.

Make sure you put waxed paper on the counter before you start sifting. It will make cleanup a lot easier!

"You mean like when I sift through the garbage looking for lunch?" asked Pig.

"I can do that!" said Iguana. And he dived into the flour, throwing it everywhere!

"No, no, no," said Rooster. "Don't sift the flour like that. Put it through this sifter." Rooster turned the crank and sifted the flour into a big pile.

"Can I taste the pile?" asked Pig.

"Not yet, Pig," said Turtle. "Now we measure the flour."

"I can do that!" said Iguana. He grabbed a ruler. "The flour is four inches tall."

"No, no, no," said Rooster. "We don't want to know how *tall* it is. We want to know how *much* there is. We measure the flour with this metal measuring cup."

"We need two cups," added Turtle. "So fill it twice."

Rooster dumped the two cups of flour into the bowl.

"Can I taste it *now*?" asked Pig.

"Not yet, Pig," said Turtle. "Next we add two tablespoons of sugar, one tablespoon of baking powder, and one-half teaspoon of salt."

**Compare and Contrast**
How is Pig different from Rooster?

Measuring cups for dry ingredients are made of metal or plastic and usually come in sets of four—1 cup, 1/2 cup, 1/3 cup, and 1/4 cup. Pick the measuring cup that holds the amount you need, then dip it into the dry ingredient, getting a heaping amount. Level it off with the straight edge of a knife and let the extra fall back into the container (although Pig would be very happy if just a little fell on the floor!).

Dry ingredients can be measured in cups or grams.

*1 cup = 227 grams*

*2 cups = 454 grams*

Some ingredients are included for flavor, but not baking powder. Even Pig thinks it tastes terrible! When baking powder is added to the shortcake, bubbles of gas form and get bigger while the cake bakes, which makes it rise.

Dry ingredients are all sifted together so they will be evenly mixed.

"I can do that!" said Iguana. He looked under the table. "But where are the tablespoons?" He looked in the teapot. "No teaspoons in here!"

"No, no, no," said Rooster. "Don't look in the teapot or under the table! These spoons are for measuring. Each holds a certain amount." Rooster measured the sugar, baking powder, and salt, poured them into the big bowl, then sifted all the dry ingredients together.

Iguana wasn't far off when he looked for tablespoons under the table and teaspoons in the teapot. Tablespoons were named after the large spoons used at the table to serve soup, and teaspoons after the smaller spoons used to stir tea.

*3 teaspoons = 1 tablespoon = 14 grams*

Butter is made by churning cream, the fat in cow's milk. (This doesn't mean it comes from a fat cow!) Margarine can be used instead of butter. Butter and margarine come in sticks and are easy to measure because their wrappers are marked in tablespoons.

*1 stick butter = 1/2 cup = 8 tablespoons = 113 grams*

Butter and margarine are two types of solid shortening, or fat, used in cooking. The name "shortcake" doesn't mean the cake is short—it refers to the shortening in the recipe.

Cool butter is "cut in" to dry ingredients by using two table knives or a pastry blender. Cut the butter into tiny pieces.

"Looks awfully white in there," said Pig. "I better taste it."

"Not yet, Pig," said Turtle. "Now we add butter. We need one stick."

"I can do that!" cried Iguana. He raced outside and broke off a branch. "How's this stick?"

"No, no, no," said Rooster. "Not *that* kind of stick. A stick of *butter*." Rooster unwrapped the butter and dropped it into the bowl.

"That butter is just sitting there like a log," said Pig. "Maybe I need to taste it."

"Not yet, Pig," said Turtle. "Next we cut in the butter."

"I can do that!" said Iguana. "Uh-oh. Scissors don't cut butter very well."

"No, no, no," said Rooster. "Don't cut the butter with scissors. Use these two table knives, like this."

Rooster cut in the butter until the mixture was crumbly.

"Looks mighty dry in there," said Pig. "Perhaps I should taste it."

"Not yet, Pig," said Turtle. "Now the recipe says to beat one egg."

"I can do that!" cried Iguana.

"No, no, no," said Rooster. "Don't beat an egg with a baseball bat! We use an eggbeater." Rooster carefully broke the egg into a dish, beat it with the eggbeater, and poured it into the big bowl.

"That looks tasty," said Pig. "Please let me taste it."

"Not yet, Pig," said Turtle. "Now add milk. We need two-thirds of a cup."

Break an egg by hitting the shell gently on the edge of a countertop or bowl to make a small crack. Place both thumbs in the crack and pull the shell apart. Always crack an egg into a small bowl before you add it to the other ingredients in case the egg is bad or shell pieces fall in. Eggs add color and flavor and help hold the cake together.

You can beat eggs with a fork, a hand beater (like Rooster's), or an electric mixer. If you use an electric mixer, make sure to put the eggs in a big bowl and start off on a low speed. If you start with the mixer on high, you'll get egg on your face!

Liquid measuring cups are made of glass or plastic. Each measuring cup has a spout for pouring and extra room below the rim so you don't have to fill it to the top and worry about spilling. Always put the cup on a flat surface and measure at eye level.

Grease the pan with a solid shortening so the cake will not stick.

Rooster is mixing the batter by hand, which means to stir with a spoon instead of a mixer. (How would Iguana mix by hand?)

"I can do that!" said Iguana. "Here, hold that glass measuring cup and I'll saw off a third. We'll use the other two-thirds to measure the milk."

"Wait," said Pig. "Why don't we fill the measuring cup to the top and I'll drink down a third?"

"No, no, no," said Rooster. "The cup has marks on it—1/3—2/3—1 cup. We'll fill it to the 2/3 mark." Rooster poured the milk into the bowl.

"It surely needs tasting now!" said Pig.

"Not yet, Pig," said Turtle. "Now we mix the dough and put it in a greased baking pan." Rooster stirred and spread as Turtle read, "Bake in the oven for fifteen to eighteen minutes."

"I can do that!" cried Iguana.

Iguana shoved the pan into the oven. "Let's see, fifteen minutes equals nine hundred seconds. I'll count them. One, two, three, four—"

"No, no, no," said Rooster, and he set the timer so that Iguana would stop counting the seconds. Pig burned his tongue on the oven door trying to taste the shortcake. Turtle studied the cookbook to see what to do next.

"Let's cut up the strawberries and whip the cream," said Turtle.

Make sure you stay nearby, so you can hear the timer when your cake is ready! Cooking times are given in hours, minutes, or seconds.
*1 hour = 60 minutes*
*1 minute = 60 seconds*

Wash the strawberries first and cut off their tops. Use a cutting board and cut each strawberry in half, then cut each half in half. (How many pieces do you have now?) Watch out for your fingers!

Whipping cream comes from cow's milk. It contains more butterfat than regular cream. Iguana might think you use a whip to whip the cream, but you could use an eggbeater or electric mixer.

When you take something out of a hot oven, make sure you use a pot holder or oven mitt.

A trick to tell if your shortcake is done: Stick a toothpick or knife in the center of the cake. If it comes out clean, without any cake sticking to it, the shortcake is ready.

Don't forget to turn off the oven when you're finished!

And they cut and cut and whipped and whipped, until
... *ding!*

Rooster grabbed the oven mitt off Iguana's head and
took the shortcake carefully out of the oven.

"Oh, it's beautiful, and it smells *sooo* good," said Pig.
"I know I have to taste it now."

"Not yet, Pig," said Turtle. "We need to let it cool."

Soon the shortcake was ready to cut. Rooster sliced
it in half.

They stacked one layer of cake, one layer of whipped cream, one layer of strawberries.

Then again—cake, cream, berries.

It looked just like the picture of the strawberry shortcake in the cookbook.

"This is the most wonderful, magnificent strawberry shortcake in the whole wide world," said Rooster. "If Great-Granny could see me now! Let's take it to the table."

"I can do that!" cried Iguana.

He yanked at the plate. The shortcake tilted …
and slid …

## splat!

Right on the floor.

Pig was ready. "Now it's my turn—to taste it!"

In a split second the strawberry shortcake was
gone. Every last crumb had disappeared into the
potbelly of the pig.

"Our shortcake!" Iguana cried. "You ate it!"

"I thought it was my turn," replied Pig. "I'm the
taster, remember? And it tasted great!"

"But it was our **masterpiece**," moaned Turtle.

"And a **tasty** one, too," said Pig. "Now we can
make something else."

"Yeah …" Iguana glared. "How about a plump,
juicy roast pig?"

Pig gasped. "Roast pig? How about iguana
potpie—or—or—turtle soup!"

"No, no, no!" cried Rooster. "Listen to me! We made this shortcake as a team, and teams work together."

"But Pig ate it!" whined Turtle.

"Iguana dropped it," pouted Pig.

"Turtle should have caught it," grumbled Iguana.

"It doesn't matter," said Rooster. "The first shortcake was just for practice. It won't be as hard to make the second time!"

"Well," added Turtle, "we don't have to worry about messing up the kitchen. It's already a mess."

"So, who will help me make it again?" asked Rooster.

Pig, Turtle, and Iguana looked at each other.

"I will!" said Pig.

"I will!" said Turtle.

"I will!" said Iguana.

"Cook-a-doodle-dooooo!" crowed Rooster. "Let's get cooking again!"

Together they made the second most wonderful, magnificent strawberry shortcake in the whole wide world. And it was a lot easier than the first time!

# Family Tales with Janet and Susan

**Janet Stevens and Susan Stevens Crummel**

Authors **Janet Stevens** and **Susan Stevens Crummel** were not very close when they were growing up, but now they have as much fun working together as the animals in their story did.

They are sisters who both like animals. Janet's favorite books as a child were about animals. She still reads animal stories today. Janet likes telling old tales in new ways, just as she did in this story. The sisters wrote this book together. Then Janet created the illustrations. She's been drawing ever since she was a child.

**Other books** by Janet Stevens and Susan Stevens Crummel: *Jackalope* and *And the Dish Ran Away with the Spoon*

**LOG ON** ▶ Find out more about the authors at **www.macmillanmh.com**.

### (CA) Authors' Purpose

What was the authors' purpose for writing *Cook-a-Doodle-Doo!*? Did they want to inform or entertain? How did they meet their goal?

# CA Critical Thinking

## Summarize

Summarize *Cook-a-Doodle-Doo!* Use the Venn diagram to help you compare Pig and Rooster. Compare and contrast the main characters. Use descriptions of their personalities and events in the story.

Different Alike

## Think and Compare

1. **Compare** and **contrast** Rooster's character from how he was in the beginning to how he is in the end of the story. Use details from the story in your answer. **Make Inferences and Analyze: Compare and Contrast**

2. Which character is most helpful to Rooster? Which character is least helpful? Explain why. Support your answer with information from the story. **Analyze**

3. Suppose you wanted to bake a cake. Which of the characters in the story would you ask to help you? Why? **Apply**

4. Why is it important to follow directions in **recipes**? Explain your answer. **Evaluate**

5. Read "Red and Her Friends" on pages 350–351. How is it similar to *Cook-a-Doodle-Doo!*? How are the two stories different? Use details from both stories in your answer. **Reading/Writing Across Texts**

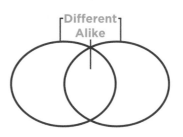

**Genre**

Nonfiction gives information about real people, places, or things.

✔ **Text Feature**

Diagrams are drawings that help you understand information in the text.

**Content Vocabulary**

schedule

sequence

ingredients

profits

# Welcome to the Bakery!

*by Eric Michaels*

Have you ever walked into a bakery and enjoyed the wonderful smells and tastes of freshly baked breads, pies, and cakes? Those baked goods are the results of truly hard work!

Most bakers get to work at three or four o'clock in the morning. They have to do that so the rolls, muffins, and breads will be ready to be sold before breakfast time.

When you think about all of the things sold at a bakery, the work of a baker seems amazing! Bread is just one of the things they make, and most bakeries make and sell many kinds. They bake white breads, whole wheat, rye breads, French breads, raisin breads, and pumpernickels.

# How Bread Is Made

## Reading a Diagram

**Follow the arrows in this diagram to see how bread is made.**

**Bakers follow these steps to make bread.**

**1** Bread ingredients are mixed in a large mixer.

**2** The dough rests and rises in a big mixing bowl.

**3** The dough is cut into loaf-sized pieces.

**4** The dough is kneaded, or pressed and stretched.

**5** The loaves of dough rest and rise again.

**6** The loaves are baked in a big oven.

**7** Fresh bread is ready!

At the start of the day, bakers organize their work **schedule**. They plan times to bake, sell, and order supplies. They also plan the **sequence** of their baking, such as what they should bake first.

### A Baker's Day

Bakers must create and mix their doughs. Every type of bread begins with a different dough. Each ingredient in the dough must be carefully weighed or measured.

Then, the **ingredients** must be mixed together. A bakery has huge mixing bowls and machines to do the mixing. After all the ingredients are mixed into a sticky dough, it must "rest" for several hours. Bread dough can't be rushed! Next, pieces of dough are cut by hand and weighed. Each piece will become one loaf of bread. But nothing is ready to be baked yet!

The dough still must be kneaded. That means that a baker must stretch it and press it over and over until it feels softer and all ingredients are completely mixed together. After kneading, the dough is shaped into loaves. Some loaves are round, some are long and thin, and others look like big braids.

It is not time to put those loaves in the oven yet! They need another "rest." Then they are finally ready to go in the oven. A bakery oven can be as big as a room. The baker watches carefully as the breads bake. When they are crusty and golden brown, the loaves are taken out of the oven to cool. Then they are ready to be sold.

## Running a Bakery

A bakery is a business, so a good baker must also be a good business person. Buying ingredients, setting prices, and figuring out **profits**, or how much money is made, are all part of the bakery business.

Running a bakery is hard work, but baking beautiful, delicious things can be fun and rewarding. After all, people are always happy to enjoy the tasty treats that bakers create!

 **Critical Thinking**

1. Look at the text and diagram on page 379. What happens before bread dough is cut into loaves? What happens after the baker kneads the dough? **Reading a Diagram**

2. What kind of a person do you think would make a good baker? Why do you think that? **Analyze**

3. Think about this article and *Cook-a-Doodle-Doo!* What tips could a real baker give the animals? **Reading/Writing Across Texts**

 **History/Social Science Activity**

Research baking recipes from other countries. Draw and label a diagram showing how to make the tastiest recipe you find. Give the diagram a title.

 Find out more at **www.macmillanmh.com**.

✓ **Character Development: Change and Growth**

Good writers show their characters changing throughout their stories.

# Reading and Writing Connection

Read the passage below. Notice how author Janet Stevens helps us see how Rooster and Turtle teach Pig and Iguana.

**An excerpt from**
*Cook-a-Doodle-Doo*

The author lets us know that both Pig and Iguana need some help with this recipe. We see that they have some things to learn.

"Not yet, Pig," said Turtle. "Next we cut the butter."

"I can do that!" said Iguana. "Uh-oh. Scissors don't cut butter very well."

"No, no, no," said Rooster. "Don't cut the butter with scissors. Use these two table knives, like this."

Rooster cut in the butter until the mixture was crumbly.

"Looks mighty dry in there," said Pig. "Perhaps I should taste it?"

"Not yet Pig," said Turtle. "Now the recipe says to beat one egg."

"I can do that," cried Iguana.

Cook-A-Doodle-Doo!

by Janet Stevens and
Susan Stevens Crummel
illustrated by Janet Stevens

## Read and Find

Read the rest of Grace's story below. How did Grace show character development? Use the Writer's Checklist to help you.

# Missing Dog
### By Grace F.

When Sarah got home, Fluffy did not run to greet her. Fluffy was missing!... Then she heard a bark that was definitely familiar. She turned around. There was Fluffy!

Read about Fluffy's bath time.

Sarah gave Fluffy a bath. She washed him completely instead of just dunking him in soapy water. She scrubbed and dried him with a towel. He was spotless.

# Writer's Checklist

 Does Sarah do anything that she has not done before?

 Does she do anything that she has done from the past but in a different way?

☑ Can you find any reason why Sarah might have learned to be more careful?

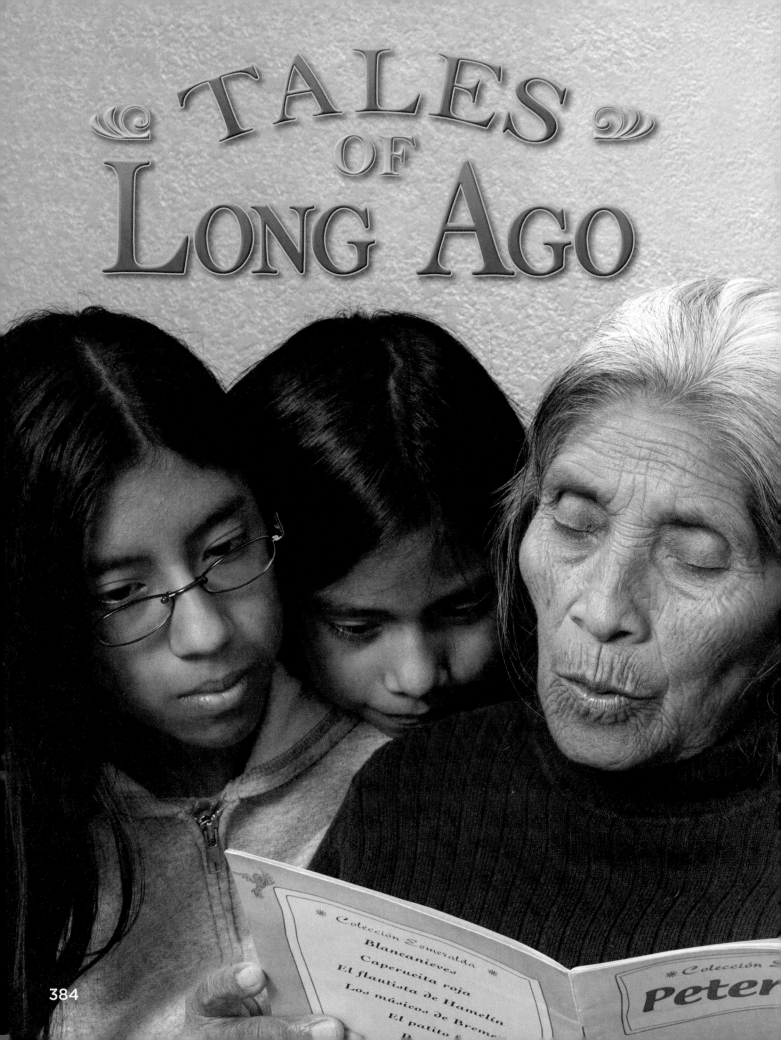

**CA** **Talk About It**

What kinds of stories do
your family and friends
pass on to one another?

**LOG ON** ▶ Find out more about fairy
tales and storytelling at
**www.macmillanmh.com**.

385

# Count On Detective Drake!

*by Arthur Stamos*

**D**etective Drake was napping with his feet up on his desk when the phone rang. He yawned and picked it up. "Hello?" he said wearily. "I'll take the case. I will **depart** at once." Drake grabbed his umbrella, which was **suitable** for the rain outside, and walked out into the noisy city.

## The Case

Drake pulled up to the police station. "We've been getting unfinished math problems in the mail," the Chief said. "They're signed 'Guessss Who?' Every day the number of letters **increases**. We keep getting more. They are clogging up the mail room."

Drake looked at the paper in the Chief's hand. He **observed** one letter's clue:

$$\square + 32 = 51 \text{ Guessss Who?}$$

**Gathering Clues**

"The word *guess* isn't spelled right," Drake said thoughtfully. "Give me the clues, Chief," he said. "And if someone asks you, say that I've **advised** you not to discuss the case. If you do what I say, I'll get this problem solved quickly."

Drake took the clues and went back to his office. First, he filled in the missing numbers. Then, he wrote the numbers in a notebook:

1 1 5 5 5 8 10 11 11 14 19 20

"Is it a code?" he thought aloud. "Think, Drake, think!" "Maybe it's an alphabet code!" Drake shouted. When he matched the numbers to the letters of the alphabet, this is what he had:

A A E E E H J K K N S T

**Case Solved!**

"This doesn't add up," he said, disappointed and **discouraged**. He kept moving the letters around. Finally, he had it: JAKE THE SNAKE.

Drake called the Chief. "That snake, Jake, is your man."

"I knew I could *count* on you!" said the Chief.

## Reread for **Comprehension**

### Analyze Story Structure

**Character, Setting, Plot** The structure of a story is made up of the setting, the characters, and the story events, or plot. The **setting** is when and where the story takes place. In some stories, such as fairy tales or historical fiction, the setting can cause characters to act in certain ways. Reread the selection and use your Setting Web to record **clues** about the setting.

**Comprehension**

## Genre

Fairy Tales take place long ago and have imaginary characters and settings.

## Analyze Story Structure

Character, Setting, Plot
Use your Setting Web.

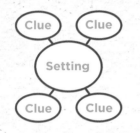

## Read to Find Out

What happens to Aziza?

# One Riddle, One Answer

by Lauren Thompson

illustrated by Linda S. Wingerter

Long ago in Persia, there lived a powerful sultan. He had many sons, but only one daughter, named Aziza, and he wished for her a wise and happy life. The finest tutors in the land were brought to the palace, and Aziza learned all there was to know. But her favorite subject was numbers. And her favorite game was riddles.

Character, Setting, Plot
When and where does this story take place?

391

The time came for Aziza to marry. The sultan began to seek a **suitable** husband for her.

"Who in the land is most worthy of her hand?" the sultan asked his advisors.

"My eldest son is very handsome, your honor," said one advisor.

"My youngest son is very clever," said another.

It seemed that all of the sultan's advisors had only their own sons to recommend. The sultan was angry.

"You have **advised** enough!" cried the sultan, and he sent his advisors away.

Then Aziza went to the sultan.

"Father," she said, "perhaps there is a better way to choose whom I should marry."

The sultan knew his daughter was wise and good, and above all he wished her to be happy. "Tell me your plan," he said.

"Let me pose a riddle," said Aziza. "The riddle has but one true answer. Whoever can answer the riddle will be the one I would be happiest to marry."

"A riddle?" asked the sultan.

"Yes," said Aziza. "Here it is."

Placed above, it makes great things small.
Placed beside, it makes small things greater.
In matters that count, it always comes first.
Where others increase, it keeps all things the same.
What is it?

The sultan thought for a moment, and then he sighed. "This riddle is too difficult even for me. In all the land, there is no man who will solve this riddle."

"Perhaps there will be one," Aziza said. "And one is all that is needed."

So the sultan agreed to Aziza's plan.

The next day, Aziza set out with a caravan in search of the one who could solve the riddle. In every city, town, and village, a messenger spread the news of the sultan's daughter's riddle.

"One riddle, one answer! Let any number try!" cried the messenger. "Only one will win the hand of the sultan's daughter!"

Every place they stopped, men young and old tried to solve the riddle. But none had the answer.

**Character, Setting, Plot**
Where does Aziza go on the caravan? Why?

In one village, a scholar came before Aziza to announce his answer. He was an astronomer, who studied the movements of the sun, moon, and stars.

"I have **observed** that the answer is the sun," he said with much confidence. "For the riddle speaks of shadows. When the sun is high above us, even the greatest man seems small, as he has only a small shadow. Thus, the answer is the sun."

"A learned answer indeed," said Aziza. "But that is not the right answer to the riddle."

In another town, a soldier came before Aziza with his answer.

"A sword!" he cried, displaying his gleaming saber. "The answer must be a sword. For the riddle speaks of war. And in war, even the smallest man is great in strength with a sword by his side."

"You have given a strong answer," said Aziza. "But that is not the right answer to the riddle."

In another city, a merchant came before Aziza.

"Honored lady," he said sweetly, "your clever riddle has been solved. The riddle speaks of the ways of the world, and the answer, therefore, is money. For as everyone knows, in all matters that count, money always comes first." He smiled at Aziza, sure that he had won her hand.

"Your answer is more clever than my riddle," said Aziza wearily. "But your clever answer is wrong."

"May I try another riddle?" asked the merchant.

"No," Aziza said. "One riddle, one answer."

Aziza felt **discouraged**. Perhaps her father was right. Perhaps no one in the land would know the answer to the riddle. She ordered the caravan to return to her father's palace.

Just as the caravan was about to **depart**, a young man came forward. He was a farmer named Ahmed, and he too loved numbers.

"Will you hear one more answer?" Ahmed asked.

"Just one more," Aziza said, sighing.

"The riddle speaks of numbers," he said, "and the answer is the number one. For in a fraction, the number one placed above a large number makes a small number. One hundred is large, but one hundredth is small."

"Yes, it is," said Aziza. "Go on."

"And when the number one is placed beside another number," he said, "the number increases. One placed beside nine makes nineteen."

"Or ninety-one," said Aziza. She smiled.

"Or ninety-one," said Ahmed. He smiled back.

"And in counting," Ahmed went on, "the number one always comes first. That is as simple as one, two, three."

"Yes!" said Aziza, laughing.

Ahmed said, "And in multiplication, the number one keeps the value of another number, while other numbers increase the value. One times ten is ten, but two times ten is twenty, and three times ten is thirty. And this is why," said Ahmed, "the answer to your riddle is the number one."

"That is a wonderful answer," said Aziza. "And it is right! With this answer, you have won my hand."

"With this riddle, you have won my heart," said Ahmed.

Aziza and Ahmed returned to the sultan's palace. Before long, they were married.

The sultan made Ahmed his chief advisor in matters of farming.

And he made Aziza his chief advisor in matters of numbers.

# By the Numbers with Lauren and Linda

Author **Lauren Thompson** is a lot like Aziza. She has loved words and numbers ever since she was a girl. Lauren put her two favorite things together to write this riddle story. She set her story in Persia (the country now called Iran) because that is where many important math ideas began.

**Other books** by Lauren Thompson: *Little Quack's Hide and Seek* and *Mouse's First Summer*

Illustrator **Linda S. Wingerter** has illustrated many books for children. Besides being an artist, Linda has another talent: she is an excellent skater, and she enjoys doing it very much.

**LOG ON** ▶ Find out more about Lauren Thompson and Linda S. Wingerter at **www.macmillanmh.com**.

 **Author's Purpose**

What was Lauren Thompson's purpose for writing *One Riddle, One Answer*? What clues can you use to figure out her purpose?

# Critical Thinking

## Summarize

Summarize Aziza's search for a husband in *One Riddle, One Answer.* Be sure to describe the characters, setting, and plot. Use your Setting Web to help you.

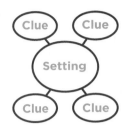

Clue  Clue
Setting
Clue  Clue

## Think and Compare

1. Why is the **setting** an important part of the **plot**? Use details from the story in your answer. **Analyze Story Structure: Character, Setting, Plot**

2. Explain why Ahmed is a **suitable** husband for Aziza. Use story details to support your answer. **Analyze**

3. If you were to meet Ahmed, what questions would you ask him? **Apply**

4. Why do people like to have friends with similar interests? Explain your answer. **Evaluate**

5. Why does Detective Drake use numbers on pages 386–387? How is this different from the way Aziza uses numbers in *One Riddle, One Answer*? Use details from both selections in your answer. **Reading/ Writing Across Texts**

## CA Language Arts

### Genre
**Fairy Tales** are stories that take place long ago and have imaginary characters and settings.

### ✔ Literary Elements
**Sensory Language** is the use of words and images that appeal to the senses.

# Beauty and the Beast

**adapted by Amy Ehrlich**

*A once wealthy merchant stumbles upon a beautiful castle in the woods. He eats, drinks, and falls asleep, but does not see the owner of the castle. He picks a rose for his daughter, Beauty. This angers the ugly beast who lives there. The beast demands that one of the merchant's daughters must now come to live the rest of her life in the castle.*

*Beauty and her father set out for the castle the next morning. A delicious meal awaits them.*

**H**ardly had they finished eating when they heard the beast's footsteps echoing on the marble floor. Beauty clung to her father in terror, but the beast spoke to them in a mild tone and inquired about their journey. "Have you come here willingly, Beauty, to die in place of your father?" he said at last.

"Yes, willingly, and I know that I must stay," she said, looking at his face and trying to keep her voice from trembling.

"That is good," the beast answered. "Your father may spend the night but must go home in the morning." He bowed and took his leave of them.

406

Beauty tried to comfort her father when they parted by saying that the beast did not seem very cruel. Perhaps he would relent and one day allow her to return home.

She watched him ride off and then walked up a curving stairway into a room with mirrors all around. On the door was written in golden letters "Beauty's Room." In the morning a clock awakened her by calling her name softly twelve times. She was alone all day, but when she was having her supper, the beast would draw the curtains and come in. He spoke to her so pleasantly that she soon lost much of her fear of him.

Each night just before he left, he turned toward her and said, "Am I very ugly?"

"Yes," replied Beauty, "but you are so kind to me that I no longer mind."

"Will you marry me then?" he asked.

"Pray do not ask me," said Beauty.

"Since you will not, then good night, Beauty." And the beast would go away.

The castle was full of galleries and apartments containing rare and precious things. In one room was a cage filled with exotic birds. In another a troop of monkeys of all sizes came to meet her, making low bows. Beauty was enchanted with them and asked the beast if she might have one to keep her company. At once, two young apes appeared and two small monkeys with them. They chattered and jumped all around her, making Beauty laugh.

Each night at suppertime, the beast came to see her. Gradually, she came to know him and liked him more and more. But to his question, "Beauty, will you marry me?" she always said, "No, Beast," very gently. And when she said these words, it seemed to her that he was sad and in some way disappointed with her.

Though Beauty had everything she could wish for and was content there, she never stopped missing her father and her brothers and sisters. At last, one evening she begged the beast to let her go home.

"Ah, Beauty, will you desert an unhappy beast so easily? Very well, then. You shall visit your home but must promise to return in two months' time. You will not need any horse to carry you back. Only take this ring and turn it twice upon your finger the night before you come away and in the morning you will be with me."

The beast told her to take all that she wanted from the castle as presents for her family and he gave her two trunks. Though Beauty heaped them to the top with gold and trinkets, there always seemed to be more room, and they were not filled until she was tired of packing them. She went to sleep, but in the morning when she awoke she was in a strange place. Suddenly, she heard her father's voice and knew that she was home.

Her sisters and brothers greeted her joyfully. But though their fortunes had changed and they were living in the town again, their entertainments seemed hollow. Beauty often thought of the castle, where she had been so happy. As the weeks went by she spoke of returning, but her father and brothers begged her to stay and she

had not the courage to say good-bye to them.

The ring the beast had given her was on her dressing stand. One night Beauty put it on and gazed into the stone. Slowly an image appeared, and she saw the beast in a far part of the castle gardens. He was lying on his back and seemed to be dying. Beauty grasped the ring and turned it around two times.

In the morning she was at the beast's castle. She searched everywhere but could not find him.

At last she ran to the place in the gardens she had dreamed of and came upon the beast lying among the high bushes. Beauty put her head down on his chest, but at first he was not breathing. Then she began to weep. "Oh, he is dead and it is on my account," she said, and her tears fell upon his face. Slowly the beast opened his eyes.

"Oh, Beast, how you frightened me!" Beauty cried. "I never before knew how much I loved you."

"Can you really care for such an ugly creature as I am?" said the beast faintly.

"Yes, oh yes, dear Beast. Only live to be my husband and I will be your wife forever."

The moment Beauty uttered these words, a dazzling light shone everywhere. The palace windows glittered as lamps lit up inside, and music was heard all around. To Beauty's great wonder a handsome prince stood before her. He said that her loving words had broken the spell of a magician who had doomed him to wear the form of a beast. This terrible enchantment could be broken only when a maiden loved him in spite of his ugliness.

Then the grateful prince claimed Beauty as his bride. He sent for her father and her brothers and sisters, and the wedding was celebrated the very next day.

## CA Critical Thinking

1. Look at the paragraph in blue on page 407. What examples of sensory language does the author use in this story? **Sensory Language**

2. In what ways do the names, Beauty and Beast, match the characters' personalities? Do the names always match their behavior? **Analyze**

3. Compare Beauty with Aziza in *One Riddle, One Answer*. What character traits do they share? **Reading/Writing Across Texts**

LOG ON ▶ Find out more about Fairy Tales at www.macmillanmh.com.

## Writing

**CA**

✓ **Character Development: Change and Growth**

Good writers write about characters that can change and learn.

Read the passage below. Notice how author Lauren Thompson shows us how Aziza feels frustrated and curious at the same time.

**An excerpt from**
***One Riddle One Answer***

The author creates a character who is trying to figure out a riddle. We watch her and wonder whether she will figure it out before she gets too discouraged and gives up.

"Will you hear one more answer?" Ahmed asked.

"Just one more," Aziza said, sighing.

"The riddle speaks of numbers," he said, "and the answer is number one. For in a fraction, the number one placed above a large number makes a small number. One hundred is large, but one hundredth is small."

"Yes, it is," said Aziza. "Go on."

410

# Read and Find

Read Henry's writing below. How did he use character development in his writing? Use the checklist below to help you.

## Tired of Waiting
### By Henry H.

Read about what happens to my little sister.

Hopping from one foot to another, Talia waits in line. A woman shoots her an unfriendly look, so she stares right back. Mom gives Talia a cold stare.

On the way to the car, Talia is wondering what her punishment will be. In the car, no one says anything at all. She sits quietly not looking at anyone.

---

## Writer's Checklist

✓ Does Talia act differently in the second paragraph than in the first paragraph?

✓ Can you guess what might have happened in between the two paragraphs?

☑ Can you guess what Talia might have learned between the first and second paragraphs?

**Review**

Make Inferences
Make Judgements
Main Idea and Details
Prefixes, Diagram

# THE NEWS
## from School

Kevin couldn't believe it when he heard the news. His second-grade teacher, Ms. Blanco, was awarded Teacher of the Year! Kevin decided to write about Ms. Blanco in the school newspaper.

After school Kevin rode his bicycle to Ms. Blanco's house. A group of radio and television reporters waited outside.

"Ms. Blanco, can I talk to you for a minute for the school paper?" asked Kevin.

"I'm sorry, Kevin. I really have no time," Ms. Blanco answered. "I was just telling these reporters that I need to go to teacher-training class."

"Class? Why? You're a teacher!" Kevin cried.

Ms. Blanco explained, "I still take classes every week. In my class I learn more about how to be a better teacher."

Ms. Blanco smiled and rushed away. "How am I ever going to get to talk to her?" wondered Kevin. He thought and thought. Finally, he knew. He would write his questions in a letter. He wrote:

Dear Ms. Blanco,

Congratulations! I'm working on the school newspaper, and I wondered if you could answer a few questions.

1. Did you always want to be a teacher?
2. Do you have any pets?
3. Do you have any hobbies?
4. What advice would you give young people who want to be teachers?

Thanks for your help!

Sincerely,
Kevin Washington

Kevin left the letter under the door of Ms. Blanco's classroom. The next day he found a note waiting for him on his desk. It read:

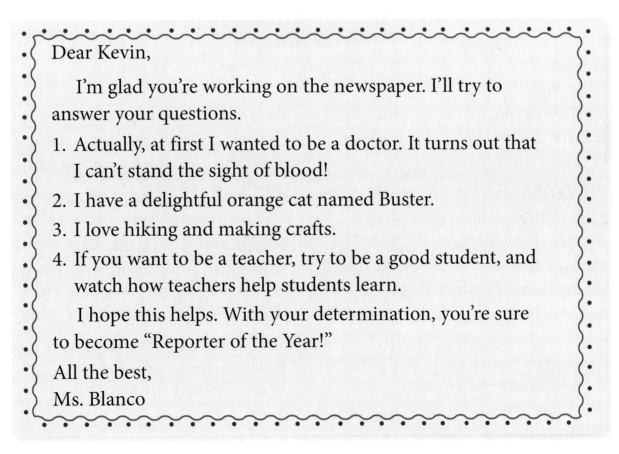

Dear Kevin,

I'm glad you're working on the newspaper. I'll try to answer your questions.

1. Actually, at first I wanted to be a doctor. It turns out that I can't stand the sight of blood!
2. I have a delightful orange cat named Buster.
3. I love hiking and making crafts.
4. If you want to be a teacher, try to be a good student, and watch how teachers help students learn.

I hope this helps. With your determination, you're sure to become "Reporter of the Year!"

All the best,
Ms. Blanco

# Venus Flytrap
## The Plant with Bite!

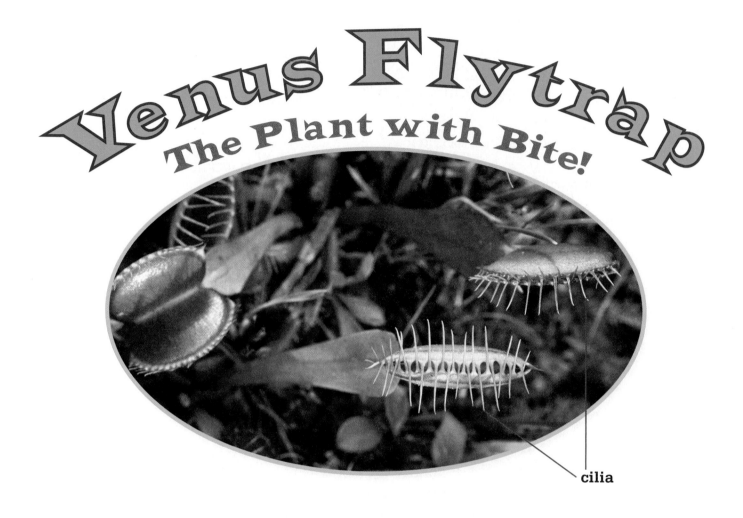

cilia

Imagine a plant that eats living things. Do you picture a plant that looks as if it came from another planet? Think again! The United States is home to a fascinating plant that eats live food, and the plant is not as strange as you might think.

You may have seen or heard of this carnivorous, or meat-eating, plant. It is called the Venus flytrap. It grows in bogs, or wetlands, near the coasts of North Carolina and South Carolina.

The Venus flytrap grows to be only about a foot tall. The plant has white flowers in the spring, but it is the plant's leaves that make it interesting. The leaves have hinged parts with stiff hairs. These are the plant's "traps."

The Venus flytrap eats flies, ants, spiders, caterpillars, crickets, and slugs. Like other plants, the Venus flytrap makes most of its food using sunshine, air, and water. Live food gives it the extra nutrition it needs to grow well in damp soil.

The Venus flytrap uses a sweet liquid called nectar to attract bugs. When a bug lands on one of the open traps, trigger hairs on the surface make the trap shut. After the trap closes, the bug is dinner!

The bristles, or cilia, along the edges of the trap come together like a shoelace so the bug cannot get out. Then the trap acts like a tiny stomach and digests the bug. Each trap catches and digests a few bugs. Then the plant replaces the used trap with a fresh, new trap.

If you want to have your own Venus flytrap at home, you have to buy a plant from a nursery. There are strict laws about taking these plants out of the wild. They cannot be removed from public land without permission.

If you are ever near the coast of North Carolina or South Carolina, you might spot a Venus flytrap. Maybe you will even see it catch a tasty bug. Yum!

# CA Critical Thinking

**Now answer Numbers 1 through 4. Base your answers on the passage "The News from School."**

**1. What does the prefix *bi-* in the word *bicycle* mean?**

  **A**  Two
  **B**  Wheel
  **C**  One half
  **D**  Vehicle

**2. Why is Kevin unable to interview Ms. Blanco in the beginning of the passage?**

  **A**  He has soccer practice.
  **B**  He has to take his little sister home.
  **C**  He has to wait for her letter.
  **D**  Ms. Blanco has to leave for her class.

**3. Why do you think Ms. Blanco is successful?**

  **A**  She is likable.
  **B**  She knows the judges.
  **C**  She is very tough.
  **D**  She has continued to work very hard at being a good teacher.

**4. What judgments can you make about Ms. Blanco based on the answers in her letter? Use details from the passage to support your answer.**

_____

_____

_____

_____

**Now answer Numbers 1 through 4. Base your answers on the passage "Venus Flytrap: The Plant with Bite!"**

**1. Which detail about Venus flytraps is NOT correct?**

A  Venus flytraps grow in swamps.

B  Venus flytraps eat mice and squirrels.

C  Venus flytraps are about a foot tall.

D  You have to buy Venus flytraps.

**2. What is the main idea of this passage?**

A  The Venus flytrap is an interesting plant that eats live bugs by trapping them in its leaves.

B  The Venus flytrap is found near the coasts of North Carolina and South Carolina.

C  The Venus flytrap is carnivorous.

D  The Venus flytrap is a dangerous plant that grows in moist areas near the coasts.

**3. According to the diagram, the cilia**

A  are found on the outside edge of the leaf.

B  are found inside the leaf next to the trigger hairs.

C  are found near the plant's stem.

D  are round.

**4. What inference can you make about the job of the trigger hairs?**

A  They help the plant receive sunlight.

B  They detect when a bug has landed on it.

C  They help the plant grow new leaves.

D  They work like a shoelace to trap the food inside the leaves.

## Write on Demand

**PROMPT** Venus flytraps are plants, but they are also hunters. Explain how the Venus flytrap catches and digests its food. What might be some advantages and disadvantages to being a carnivorous plant? Write for 15 minutes. Write as much as you can, as well as you can.

# Glossary

## What Is a Glossary?

**A** glossary can help you find the **meanings** of words in this book that you may not know. The words in the glossary are listed in **alphabetical order**. **Guide words** at the top of each page tell you the first and last words on the page.

Each word is divided into syllables. The way to pronounce the word is given next. You can understand the pronunciation respelling by using the **pronunciation key** at the right. A shorter key appears at the bottom of every other page. When a word has more than one syllable, a dark accent mark (´) shows which syllable is stressed. In some words, a light accent mark (´) shows which syllable has a less heavy stress. Sometimes an entry includes a second meaning for the word.

beamed

gnaws

## Guide Words

**First word on the page**   **Last word on the page**

## Sample Entry

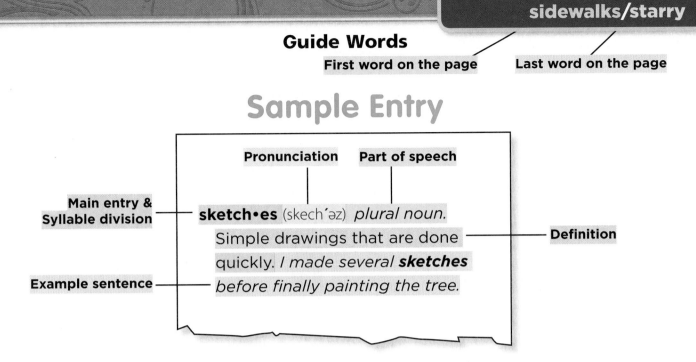

**Pronunciation**   **Part of speech**

**Main entry & Syllable division**

**sketch•es** (skech´əz) *plural noun.* Simple drawings that are done quickly. *I made several **sketches** before finally painting the tree.*

**Definition**

**Example sentence**

# Pronunciation Key

| Phonetic Spelling | Examples |
|---|---|
| a | at, bad, plaid, laugh |
| ā | ape, pain, day, break |
| ä | father, calm |
| âr | care, pair, bear, their, where |
| e | end, pet, said, heaven, friend |
| ē | equal, me, feet, team, piece, key |
| i | it, big, give, hymn |
| ī | ice, fine, lie, my |
| îr | ear, deer, here, pierce |
| o | odd, hot, watch |
| ō | old, oat, toe, low |
| ô | coffee, all, taught, law, fought |
| ôr | order, fork, horse, story, pour |
| oi | oil, toy |
| ou | out, now, bough |
| u | up, mud, love, double |
| ū | use, mule, cue, feud, few |
| ü | rule, true, food, fruit |
| ù | put, wood, should, look |
| ûr | burn, hurry, term, bird, word, courage |
| ə | about, taken, pencil, lemon, circus |
| b | bat, above, job |
| ch | chin, such, match |

| Phonetic Spelling | Examples |
|---|---|
| d | dear, soda, bad |
| f | five, defend, leaf, off, cough, elephant |
| g | game, ago, fog, egg |
| h | hat, ahead |
| hw | white, whether, which |
| j | joke, enjoy, gem, page, edge |
| k | kite, bakery, seek, tack, cat |
| l | lid, sailor, feel, ball, allow |
| m | man, family, dream |
| n | not, final, pan, knife, gnaw |
| ng | long, singer |
| p | pail, repair, soap, happy |
| r | ride, parent, wear, more, marry |
| s | sit, aside, pets, cent, pass |
| sh | shoe, washer, fish, mission, nation |
| t | tag, pretend, fat, dressed |
| th | thin, panther, both |
| th | these, mother, smooth |
| v | very, favor, wave |
| w | wet, weather, reward |
| y | yes, onion |
| z | zoo, lazy, jazz, rose, dogs, houses |
| zh | vision, treasure, seizure |

419

# Aa

**ad•just** (ə just′) *verb*. To arrange or change to fit. *The truck driver had to **adjust** his seat to get comfortable.*

**ad•vised** (ad vīzd′) *verb*. Offered ideas about solving a problem. *The dentist **advised** me to brush more often to prevent cavities.*

**af•fec•tion** (ə fek′ shən) *noun*. A tender feeling; sentiment. *Hugging is a common way to express **affection**.*

**a•gree•a•ble** (ə grē′ə bəl) *adjective*. Nice; pleasant. *The flowers in the room had an **agreeable** smell.*

**a•larmed** (ə lärmd′) *verb*. To suddenly fear approaching danger. *The zoo keeper was **alarmed** to find the lion cage door ajar.*

## Word History

**Alarm** comes from Old French *alarme* and Italian *all'arme,* "to arms!"

**an•xious** (āngk′ shəs, āng′ shəs) *adjective*. 1. Feeling of dread. 2. Excited in anticipation. *1. Robert was **anxious** about his test scores. 2. The team was **anxious** to begin the game.*

**ar•chi•tects** (är′ki tekts′) *plural noun*. People who design buildings and supervise their construction. *A group of **architects** showed up at the empty lot and began planning the building they wanted to make there.*

**ar•gued** (är′gūd) *verb*. Disagreed or had a difference of opinion. *The two men **argued** about who had caused the accident.*

**a•ware•ness** (ə wâr′ nes) *noun*. Knowing or being mindful. *When hiking, it is important to practice **awareness**, or you may walk past an animal without seeing it.*

**ax•is** (ak′sis) *noun*. A real or imaginary straight line through the center of a spinning object. *Earth spins on its imaginary **axis**.*

# Bb

**ban•quet** (bang´kwit) *noun.* A large meal presented for an important event or date. *My soccer team has a* **banquet** *at the end of the season.*

### Word History

**Banquet** comes from the Old French word *banc,* meaning "little bench." From there it progressed to mean "meal taken on the family workbench," and then it became "feast."

**beamed** (bēmd) *verb.* 1. Shined brightly. 2. Smiled brightly. *1. The sun* **beamed** *down on the field. 2. Marleigh* **beamed** *when she thought about the joke Raffi told yesterday.*

**be•hav•ior** (bi hāv´ yər) *noun.* A manner in which something acts under a set of circumstances. *The substitute teacher was pleased by the students'* **behavior**.

**boast•ing** (bōs´ting) *verb.* Talking with too much pride. *Everyone got annoyed when Lisa started* **boasting** *about her new bicycle.*

**bril•liance** (bril´ yəns) *noun.* The state of being bright with light or luster. *The janitor was blinded by the bright* **brilliance** *of the clean tile.*

# Cc

**cha•pa•tis** (chə´pä ´tēs) *plural noun.* Flat bread. *The restaurant served fresh* **chapatis** *with the main course.*

at; āpe; fär; câre; end; mē; it; īce; pîerce; hot; ōld; sông; fôrk; oil; out; up; ūse; rüle; pùll; tûrn; chin; sing; shop; thin; this; hw in white; zh in treasure.

The symbol ə stands for the unstressed vowel sound in about, taken, pencil, lemon, and circus.

**com•mu•ni•cate** (kə mū′ ni kāt′) *verb.* To make known by information exchange. *To **communicate** his ideas, Douglas wrote in his blog.*

**com•pass** (kum′ pəs) *noun.* An instrument used to determine direction. *All hikers and campers should carry a **compass** in case they get lost.*

**con•stel•la•tions** (kon′stəl ā′shənz) *plural noun.* A group of stars forming a pattern. *Of the many **constellations**, Orion has always been Ben's favorite.*

**con•tain** (kən tān′) *verb.* To hold inside. *The storage boxes **contain** clothes.*

**con•ver•sa•tion** (kon′vər sā′shən) *noun.* A talk between two or more people. *He always enjoyed their **conversation** whenever she came to visit.*

**cross** (krôs) *adjective.* Bad tempered or peevish. *The piano teacher was **cross** with Maria because she was late again.*

**cru•cial** (krü′ shəl) *adjective.* The important factor that helps drive an action or decision. *Before buying a house, it is **crucial** to have it inspected.*

**cun•ning** (kun′ ing) *adjective.* Clever. *The **cunning** fox evaded the hounds.*

**cu•ri•os•i•ty** (kyùr′ē os′ i tē) *noun.* A rare, unusual, or strange object. *A typewriter is a **curiosity** in a world of computers.*

# Dd

**dark•ened** (där′kənd) *adjective.* Made or became blacker, so there is less light. *The **darkened** room looked scary.*

**de•ci•sions** (di sizh′ ənz) *plural noun.* Acts of making up one's mind. *The President must make many **decisions** during the course of a day.*

**dec•o•rat•ed** (dek′ə rāt′əd) *adjective.* Made to look better by adding pretty things to it. *The table was **decorated** with colorful flowers.*

**de•part** (di pärt′) *verb.* To leave or go away. *The bus will **depart** at 7:00 A.M.*

**dip•per** (dip′ ər) *noun.* A cup-like container. *The cowboy used the **dipper** to fill his canteen.*

**dis•cour•aged** (dis kûr′ijd) *adjective.* Having little or no hope. *Brad felt **discouraged** after losing the first race.*

**down** (doun) *1. noun. 2. adverb.* 1. Fine, soft feathers. 2. From a higher to a lower place. *1. During cold winter nights, the best way to stay warm is under a quilt filled with **down**. 2. The boy's mother told him to get **down** from the tree.*

# Ee

**ech•oes** (ek´ōz) *verb.* Repeats a sound. *I can hear the bird's screech as it **echoes** across the valley.*

## Word History

In Greek mythology, Echo was a beautiful maiden whose longtime love for Narcissus caused her body to weaken so much that only her voice remained.

**em•pha•size** (em´ fə sīz´) *verb.* To stress. *The coach would **emphasize** the importance of stretching before we began our workout.*

**es•sen•tial** (i sen´ shəl) *adjective.* Very important or necessary. *It is **essential** for any scuba diver to be able to swim.*

**ex•haust•ed** (ig zôs´ tid) *adjective.* Tired; depleted. *After the race, the runner was **exhausted**.*

# Ff

**fab•ric** (fab´rik) *noun.* A material made from fibers, such as cotton, silk, or nylon. *My mother bought the **fabric** to make our costumes.*

## Word History

Fabric has a complicated history, from the Latin *faber,* meaning "workman," and *fabrica,* "craft" or "workshop," to the Old French *fabrique,* and finally to the Middle English *fabryke,* which meant "something constructed."

at; āpe; fär; câre; end; mē; it; īce; pîerce; hot; ōld; sông; fôrk; oil; out; up; ūse; rüle; pu̇ll; tûrn; chin; sing; shop; thin; **th**is; hw in white; zh in treasure.

The symbol ə stands for the unstressed vowel sound in about, taken, pencil, lemon, and circus.

**fe•males** (fē′ mālz′) *adjective.* Of or relating to the sex that bears young. *Females of many bird species have feathers that are dull when compared with the males.*

**fierce** (fîrs) *adjective.* Very strong or violent. *The **fierce** hurricane affected the whole state.*

## Word History

**Fierce** comes from Latin *ferus*, meaning "wild" or "untamed."

# Gg

**gaze** (gāz) *1. verb. 2. noun.* 1. To look at for a long time. 2. A long, steady look or stare. *1. I like to **gaze** at the ocean because the waves make me calm. 2. Her curious **gaze** made him wonder if they knew each other.*

## Word History

The word **gaze** comes from Scandanavia in 1386, borrowing from *gasa*, "to gape."

**gnaws** (nôz) *verb.* Bites something hard again and again in order to wear away little by little. *My dog **gnaws** on bones all day.*

**guar•an•tee** (gar′ ən tē′) *1. noun. 2. verb.* 1. A pledge of a certain outcome. 2. To make sure or certain. *1. Susan gave her boss a **guarantee** that the work would be finished on time. 2. The company will **guarantee** that you will be satisfied with its service.*

**guests** (gests) *plural noun.* People who come to visit or to eat a meal. *The **guests** arrived for the party just before dinner.*

# Hh

**heart•y** (här′ tē) *adjective.* 1. Full of affection. 2. Enthusiastic, unrestrained. 3. Nourishing. *The farmer patted his belly after eating a portion of the hearty stew.*

**hud•dle** (hud′əl) *1. noun. 2. verb.* 1. A group of people or animals close together. 2. To gather close together in a bunch. *1. The puppies were cold, so they snuggled together in a huddle. 2. During the winter fire drill, the students had to huddle up to keep warm.*

# Ii

**i•den•ti•cal** (ī den′ ti kəl) *adjective.* Alike or similar in every way. *The identical twins were often mistaken for one another.*

**in•crease** (in krēs′) *verb.* To make bigger or greater. *Each year, we increase the size of the garden by adding a row of flowers or plants.*

**in•di•vid•u•al** (in′də vij′ü əl) *adjective.* Single; separate. *The coffee was served with individual packets of sugar.*

**in•gre•di•ent** (in grē′dē ənt) *noun, pl.* **in•gre•di•ents.** Any one of the parts used in a recipe or mixture. *The baker was missing one ingredient for making a cake.*

**in•sight•ful** (in sīt′ fəl) *adjective.* Having or showing unique perception. *The foreign speaker was very insightful.*

**in•ter•rupt•ed** (in′tər up′təd) *verb.* Broke in upon or stopped something or someone. *A loud car alarm interrupted our teacher from speaking.*

## Word History

**Interrupt** combines two Latin words, *inter,* meaning "between," and *rumpere,* "to break" or "rupture."

at; āpe; fär; câre; end; mē; it; īce; pîerce; hot; ōld; sông; fôrk; oil; out; up; ūse; rüle; půll; tûrn; chin; sing; shop; thin; **th**is; hw in white; zh in treasure.

The symbol ə stands for the unstressed vowel sound in about, taken, pencil, lemon, and circus.

**in•ves•ti•gate** (in ves′ ti gāt′) *verb.* To examine systematically. *The police were called to **investigate** the disturbance.*

# Jj

**jun•ior** (jün′yər) *adjective* The younger or smaller of two. *Ralphie was a **junior** version of his father, Clancy.*

# Kk

**kim•chi** (kim′ chē) *noun.* A spicy pickled Korean dish, usually with cabbage. *The **kimchi** was served along with many other appetizers.*

# Mm

**mag•nif•i•cent** (mag nif′ə sənt) *adjective.* Very beautiful and grand. *We walked through the **magnificent** garden and admired all the beautiful flowers.*

**ma•jor•i•ty** (mə jôr′ i tē) *noun.* The greater number of a part. *The **majority** of the class voted to have pizza rather than hamburgers.*

**man•aged** (man′ ijd) *verb.* Controlled or guided an operation. *The supervisor **managed** the project with ease.*

**mas•ter•piece** (mas′tər pēs′) *noun.* 1. A great work of art. 2. Something done with great skill. *1. The painting Mona Lisa by Da Vinci is thought to be a **masterpiece**. 2. Her plan to surprise her brother on his birthday was a **masterpiece**.*

# Nn

**North Star** (nôrth stär) *noun.* Polaris, a star. *The **North Star** is the brightest star in the Big Dipper constellation.*

# Oo

**ob•served** (əb zûrvd′) *verb.* Learned by studying someone or something. *The students **observed** the change in the plant's growth over the past three weeks.*

**o•dor** (ō′ dər) *noun.* Scent of an object. *The **odor** of the ripened bananas filled the kitchen.*

# Pp

**per•son•al•i•ty** (pûr′sə nal′i tē) *noun.* All the qualities, traits, habits, and behavior of a person. *It was in her **personality** to always be cheerful.*

**plead•ed** (plēd′ ed) *verb.* Made an earnest request. *The baby-sitter **pleaded** to the children to eat their entire dinner.*

**pol•lu•tion** (pə lü′ shən) *noun.* Harmful material introduced into an environment. *The town organized efforts to stop the **pollution** of the lake caused by the nearby factories.*

**pos•ses•sions** (pə zesh•ənz) *plural noun.* Things that are owned by someone. *Many of his **possessions** were stolen by thieves who broke into his house.*

**prep•a•ra•tions** (prep′ə rā′ shənz) *plural noun.* The act of making ready. *The **preparations** for the party included setting out flowers and appetizers.*

---

at; āpe; fär; câre; end; mē; it; īce; pîerce; hot; ōld; sông; fôrk; oil; out; up; ūse; rüle; pull; tûrn; chin; sing; shop; thin; **this**; hw in white; zh in treasure.

The symbol ə stands for the unstressed vowel sound in about, taken, pencil, lemon, and circus.

**pre•tend** (pri tend′) *verb.* To give a false appearance. *Kids love to **pretend** they are someone or something else.*

**pro•fits** (prof′ itz) *plural noun.* The outcome of gain or benefit. *The investor was pleased with the **profits** made this year.*

**pur•chased** (pûr′chəst) *verb.* Got something by paying money for it. *Lester's mother **purchased** an assortment of peppers at the store to make her salsa.*

# Qq

**quar•rel•ing** (kwôr′əl ing) *verb.* Having a heated argument. *My uncles were always **quarreling** about which baseball team was better.*

# Rr

**re•build** (rē bild′) *verb.* To repair or reassemble. *Jeff and Susan had to **rebuild** their barn after strong winds destroyed it.*

**rec•i•pes** (res′ə pēz′) *plural noun.* Lists of ingredients and instructions for making something to eat or drink. *My mother has many cookie **recipes**.*

**re•lat•ed** (ri lā′ tid) *adjective.* Connected to. *Derek was fascinated by dinosaurs and **related** subjects.*

**re•search** (ri sûrch′ or rē′sûrch′) *noun.* A careful study or investigation in order to learn facts. *A lot of **research** had to be done before the paper could be written.*

## Word History

**Research** comes from old French *recerchier*, which means "to search closely."

**re•spon•si•ble** (ri spon′ sə bəl) *adjective.* Accountable for a job or task. *Ramona's parents made her **responsible** for feeding the new puppy.*

**re•treats** (ri trēts′) *1. verb. 2. plural noun.* 1. Goes back or withdraws, as from danger. 2. Places to go to for safety, peace, and comfort. *1. A tigress **retreats** when it realizes it is outnumbered. 2. Staying in **retreats** was a helpful way for Bob to leave his problems behind him.*

**ro•tates** (rō′tāts) *verb.* Turns around. *Each planet **rotates** on its axis at a unique speed.*

# Ss

**sched•ule** (skej′ ül) *noun.* A list of times when certain events are to take place. *Teresa checked the bus **schedule** before leaving the house.*

## Word History

**Schedule** has a long history: starting with the Greek *skhida*, "to split"; the Latin *scida*, "papyrus strip"; and the Old French *cedule* and Middle English *secule*, which both mean "slip of parchment" or "paper, note."

**scram•bled** (skram′ bəld) *verb.* Moved or climbed quickly. *We all **scrambled** to the finish line in the three-legged race.*

**se•cur•ing** (si kyur′ ing) *verb.* Attaching or tying something so it does not move. *By **securing** the flashlight to the tent pole, he was able to chop firewood with both hands.*

at; āpe; fär; câre; end; mē; it; īce; pîerce; hot; ōld; sông; fôrk; oil; out; up; ūse; rüle; pùll; tûrn; chin; sing; shop; thin; **th**is; hw in white; zh in treasure.

The symbol ə stands for the unstressed vowel sound in about, taken, pencil, lemon, and circus.

**seized** (sēzd) *verb.* Took hold of or grabbed. *The guard **seized** the money out of the thief's hand.*

**se•quence** (sē′ kwəns) *noun.* The order in which things occur. *Marla's little sister recounted her entire day in **sequence**.*

**shal•low** (shal′ō) *adjective.* Not deep. *All the young children were playing in the **shallow** part of the pool.*

**shel•ter** (shel′tər) *noun.* Something that covers or protects. *The pup sought **shelter** in its den until its mother returned from the hunt.*

**shuf•fles** (shuf′əlz) *verb.* Walks without lifting the feet off the ground. *My little brother **shuffles** when he doesn't want to go somewhere.*

**sight** (sīt) *noun.* The power of vision. *Mr. Jacobs went to the eye doctor to check his **sight**.*

**source** (sôrs) *noun.* The location from which something derives. *The **source** of the brook was a spring that bubbled down the side of the mountain.*

**spe•cia•list** (spesh′ ə list) *noun.* A person who devotes himself or herself to a particular subject. *The farmer called a tree **specialist** when his apple trees failed to produce fruit.*

**sphere** (sfîr) *noun.* A round, three-dimensional shape; a globe. *Each planet is a **sphere** that revolves around the sun.*

**struc•tures** (struk′chərz) *plural noun.* Things that are built, such as buildings. *From so far away, the **structures** on the horizon were hard to make out.*

## Word History

**Structure** comes from the Latin word *struere*, which means "to heap up, build, or construct."

**suit•a•ble** (sü′tə bəl) *adjective.* Proper or right. *A new paintbrush is a **suitable** gift for my art teacher.*

**sur•vive** (sər vīv′) *verb.* To remain alive. *Although the winters are harsh, most animals and plants are able to **survive** through adaptation.*

**sym•bol** (sim'bəl) *noun.* A picture or shape that stands for something else. *A heart is a **symbol** for love.*

### Word History

The word **symbol** is derived from the Greek word *symbolon*, meaning "token" or "sign."

# Tt

**tast•y** (tās'tē) *adjective.* Having a pleasant flavor. *The freshly baked brownies were very **tasty**.*

**tech•nique** (tek nēk') *noun.* A way or method of accomplishing something. *The chef used a **technique** of cutting vegetables that was both safe and fast.*

### Word History

**Technique** comes from the Greek word *teknikos*, meaning "relating to an art or craft."

**tor•til•las** (tôr tē' yəz) *plural noun.* A thin bread made of corn or flour. *Tacos are made using corn **tortillas**.*

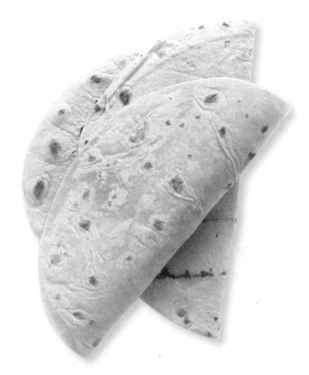

**tra•di•tion** (trə dish' ən) *noun.* The handing down of knowledge, beliefs, or customs. *It was **tradition** for Frederick's grandmother to make a pumpkin pie for Thanksgiving.*

---

at; āpe; fär; câre; end; mē; it; īce; pîerce; hot; ōld; sông; fôrk; oil; out; up; ūse; rüle; pull; tûrn; chin; sing; shop; thin; this; hw in white; zh in treasure.

The symbol ə stands for the unstressed vowel sound in about, taken, pencil, lemon, and circus.

# Uu

**un•for•tu•nate•ly** (un fôr′ chə nit lē) *adverb.* In an unlucky or unfavorable manner. **Unfortunately** *for David, it was raining on his only day off.*

**u•nique** (ū nēk′) *adjective.* 1. Being unsurpassed. 2. Being the only one of its kind. *1. Nancy made hats that were absolutely* **unique**. *2. Each family member has a unique personality.*

**un•pre•dict•a•ble** (un′pri dik′ tə bəl) *adjective.* Not to be foreseen. *The tornado was especially dangerous because its direction was so* **unpredictable**.

**un•trust•ing** (un trust′ing) *adjective.* Having doubt about something. *The* **untrusting** *neighbor did not open his door.*

**u•ti•lize** (yū′tə līz′) *verb.* To put to good use. *The marathon organizer will* **utilize** *all volunteers that show up before the race.*

# Vv

**ven•om** (ven′ əm) *noun.* 1. Poisonous fluid. 2. Spite or malice. *1. The snake's* **venom** *was dangerous to small animals, but not to humans. 2. The mean woman spoke with* **venom** *in her voice.*

# Ww

**weak•est** (wēk′est) *adjective.* Least strong or powerful. *I feel* **weakest** *in the early morning, right before eating breakfast.*

# Acknowledgments

*The publisher gratefully acknowledges permission to reprint the following copyrighted material:*

"A lonely sparrow" by Kazue Mizumura from POEM-MAKING: WAYS TO BEGIN WRITING POETRY by Myra Cohn Livingston. Copyright © 1999 by Myra Cohn Livingston. Reprinted with permission by HarperCollins Children's Books, a division of HarperCollins Publishers.

"Animal Homes" by Ann O. Squire. Copyright © 2001 by Children's Press®, a Division of Scholastic Inc. All rights reserved. Reprinted by permission.

"Antarctic Anthem" by Judy Sierra, illustrations by Jose Aruego and Ariane Dewey from ANTARCTIC ANTICS by Judy Sierra. Text copyright © 1998 by Judy Sierra. Illustrations copyright © 1998 by Jose Aruego and Ariane Dewey. Reprinted with permission by Gulliver Books, Harcourt Brace and Company.

"Beauty and the Beast" is from THE RANDOM HOUSE BOOK OF FAIRY TALES adapted by Amy Ehrlich. Copyright © 1985 by Amy Ehrlich. Reprinted by permission of Random House, Inc.

"Broken and broken" by Chosu, translated by Harry Behn, from "Cricket Song: Japanese Haiku Translated" by Harry Behn. Copyright © 1964 by Harry Behn. Copyright renewed © 1992 by Prescott Behn, Pamela Behn Adam, and Peter Behn. Used by permission of Marian Reiner. Compilation and introduction from LIGHT-GATHERING POEMS edited by Liz Rosenberg. Compilation and introduction copyright © 2000 by Liz Rosenberg. Reprinted with permission by Henry Holt and Company, LLC.

"Cook-a-Doodle Doo!" by Janet Stevens and Susan Stevens Crummel, illustrations by Janet Stevens. Text copyright © 1999 by Janet Stevens and Susan Stevens Crummel. Illustrations copyright © 1999 by Janet Stevens. Reprinted with permission of Harcourt Brace & Company.

"In a Neighborhood in Los Angeles" is from CUERPO EN LLAMAS/ BODY IN FLAMES by Francisco X. Alarcón. Reprinted with permission by Chronicle Books.

"Nacho and Lolita" by Pam Muñoz Ryan and illustrated by Claudia Rueda. Text copyright © 2005 by Pam Muñoz Ryan. Illustrations copyright © 2005 by Claudia Rueda. Used with permission of Scholastic Press, an imprint of Scholastic Inc.

"One Riddle, One Answer" by Lauren Thompson, illustrations by Linda S. Wingerter. Text copyright © 2001 by Lauren Thompson. Illustrations copyright © 2001 by Linda S. Wingerter. All rights reserved. Reprinted with permission of Scholastic Press, a division of Scholastic, Inc.

"Penguin Chick" by Betty Tatham, illustrations by Helen K. Davie. Text copyright © 2002 by Betty Tatham. Illustrations copyright © 2002 by Helen K. Davie. Reprinted with permission by HarperCollins Children's Books, a division of HarperCollins Publishers.

"Ramona and Her Father" by Beverly Cleary. Copyright © 1977 by Beverly Cleary. Reprinted by permission of HarperCollins.

"Seven Spools of Thread: A Kwanzaa Story" by Angela Shelf Medearis, illustrations by Daniel Minter. Text copyright © 2000 by Angela Shelf Medearis. Illustrations copyright © 2000 by Daniel Minter. Reprinted with permission by Albert Whitman & Company.

"Shiny colored tents" by Myra Cohn Livingston from CRICKET NEVER DOES by Myra Cohn Livingston. Text copyright © 1997 by Myra Cohn Livingston. Reprinted with permission by Margaret K. McElderry Books, an imprint of Simon & Schuster Children's Publishing Division.

"Sky Bear" is from THE EARTH UNDER SKY BEAR'S FEET: NATIVE AMERICAN POEMS OF THE LAND by Joseph Bruchac, illustrations by Thomas Locker. Text copyright © 1995 by Josheph Bruchac. Illustration copyright © 1995 by Thomas Locker. Used by permission of The Putnam & Grosset Group.

"Stone Soup" by Jon J Muth. Copyright © 2003 by Jon J Muth. Reprinted with permission of Scholastic Press, a division of Scholastic Inc.

"The Story of the First Woodpecker" by Florence Holbrook from THE BOOK OF NATURE MYTHS FOR CHILDREN. Copyright © 1977 by Houghton Mifflin Company. Reprinted with permission by Houghton Mifflin Company.

"The Strongest One" by Joseph Bruchac from PUSHING UP THE SKY: SEVEN NATIVE AMERICAN PLAYS FOR CHILDREN by Joseph Bruchac. Text copyright © 2000 by Joseph Bruchac. Reprinted with permission by Dial Books for Young Readers, a division of Penguin Putnam Inc.

"Unique Animals of the Southwest" by Tanya Lee Stone. Copyright © 2005 by Thomsno Gale, a part of The Thomson Corporation. Reprinted with permission by Blackbirch Press.

"Wilbur's Boast" by E.B. White, illustrations by Garth Williams from CHARLOTTE'S WEB. Text copyright © 1952 by E.B. White. Text copyright © renewed 1980 by E.B. White. Illustrations copyright © renewed 1980 by Estate of Garth Williams. Reprinted with permission by HarperCollins Publishers, a division of HarperCollins Publishers.

**ILLUSTRATIONS**
**Cover Illustration:** Leland Klanderman

10–33: Daniel Minter. 40–41: Anthony Lewis. 42–63: Claudia Rueda. 64–65: Stephanie Langley. 82–83: Karen Stormer Brooks. 84–105: Ilene Richard. 128–129: Thomas Locker. 132–133: Sally Springer. 216–229: Garth Williams. 230–231: Nicole Rutten. 262–265: Fomina. 268–269: Barbara Spurll. 282–303: Jon J Muth. 312–313: Cindy Revell. 314–329: Lucia Angela Perez. 340–341: Julia Woolf. 350–351: Shane McGowan. 352–377: Janet Stevens. 388–405: Linda S. Wingerter. 406–409: Sue Todd. 412: Philomena O'Neil.

**PHOTOGRAPHY**
All Photographs are by Ken Cavanagh or Ken Karp for Macmillan/ McGraw Hill (MMH) except as noted below:

Inside front and back cover: MedioImages/Getty Images. v: (t) Elena Rooraid/Photo Edit; (b) NASA. vi: Diana L. Stratton/Tom Stack and Associates. vii: (t) Karl Ammann/NPL/Minden Pictures; (b) Robert Franz/Jupiter Images. ix: Tim Graham/Getty Images. 2-3: Golden Pixels LLC/Alamy. 3: Brand X/JupiterImages. 4: Radius Images/Alamy. 5: Bettmann/CORBIS. 6-7: Masterfile Royalty Free. 8: (tr) Myrleen Ferguson Cate/Photo Edit; (bl) Richard Hutchings/PhotoEdit. 9: Myrleen Ferguson Cate/PhotoEdit. 32: (tl) Courtesy Angela Meaderis; (cr) Courtesy Daniel Minter. 34: Don Farrall/Getty Images. 35: Douglas Pulsipher/Alamy. 37: Randy Faris/CORBIS. 38-39: M Stock/Alamy. 62: (tr) Courtesy Pam Muûoz Ryan; (cr) Courtesy Claudia Rueda. 67: Ryam McVay/Getty Images, Inc. 68-69: Elena Rooraid/Photo Edit. 70: (t to b) courtesy of CFK; Beth Ann Kutchma/courtesy of CFK. 71: (tl to cr) AP Photo; Hulton Archive/Getty Images/Newscom; Novastock/Photo Edit. 72: Jupiter Images. 73: AP Photo/Alan Diaz. 74: David Young-Wolff/ Photo Edit. 75: AP Photo/City of Los Angeles/Rene Macura. 76: Ben Baker/Redux. 79: (t) Ana de Sousa/Shutterstock (c) PhotoLink/Getty Images (b) Tracy Montana/PhotoLink/Getty Images. 80-81: Blend/ PunchStock. 104: Christina Koci Hernandez/San Francisco Chronicle/ Corbis. 109: Michael Newman/Photo Edit Inc. 110-111: NASA/Dembinsky Photo Associates. 112-113: Charles O'Rear/CORBIS. 113: Steve Dunwell. 114: NASA. 114-115: NASA-JPL. 115: NASA. 116-117: (l) NASA; (bkgd) NASA-HQ-GRIN. 117: (tr) Bill Frymire/Masterfile; (bl) NASA-JSC;(bc) NASA-JSC; (br) NASA-JSC. 118:(cl, bl,br,cr) NASA-JSC. 118-119: (b) NASA-MSFC;(t) NASA, ESA. 119: NASA. 120: (br) NASA; (t) NASA. 120-121: NASA-JPL. 121: NASA. 122:NASA. 122-123: NASA-MSFC. 123: NASA. 124: NASA. 124-125: NASA,ESA.125: NASA-MSFC. 126: Courtesy of Liane B. Onish. 126-127: NASA-MSFC. 127: (tc) NASA; (b) NASA. 130: (b) NASA-JPL. 131: Donna Day/CORBIS. 135: (bl) Library of Congress; (cr) Bettmann/CORBIS. 138-139: Stephen Frink Collection / Alamy. 139: David A. Northcott/CORBIS. 140: Digital Vision/PunchStock . 141: San Diego Historical Society. 142-143: Steve Bloom Images/Alamy. 144: (bl) A.N.T./Photo Researchers, Inc; (bc) PhotoLink/Getty Images, Inc. 145: Wolfgang Kaehler/CORBIS. 166: (t) Image: Alex Lowy/lowyphoto.com Courtesy Betty Tatham; (c) Courtesy Helen K. Davie; (bl) Johnny Johnson/Animals Animals; (br) Art Wolfe/Photo Researchers. 168-169: Digital Vision/Getty Images, Inc. 171: Ryan McVay/Photodisc/Punchstock. 172-173: Mitsuhiko Imamori/ Minden Pictures. 174: (tr) Gerry Ellis/Minden Pictures; (bl) Adam Wolfitt/CORBIS. 175: (tl) Pat O'Hara/CORBIS; (cr) Joe McDonald/CORBIS.

# Acknowledgments

176-177: Diana L. Stratton/Tom Stack and Associates. 178: Fritz Polking/ Peter Arnold, Inc. 179: (c) Ken Cavanagh /Photo Researchers, Inc; (cr) Scott Camazine/Photo Researchers, Inc. 180: Jerry L. Ferrara/Photo Researchers, Inc. 181: (c) John D. Cunningham/Visuals Unlimited; (bc) Leonard Lee Roe III/Photo Researchers, Inc. 182: SuperStock, Inc./ SuperStock. 183: David Hosking. 184: (tl) Mark Boulton/Photo Researchers, Inc; (br) Kjell B. Sandved/Visuals Unlimited. 185:(tr) Bruce M. Herman/Photo Researchers, Inc; (tl) SuperStock, Inc./SuperStock; (c) Michael Giannechini/Photo Researchers, Inc. 186: Glen Oliver/Visuals Unlimited. 187: E. R. Degginger. 188: (tl) Jeff Lepone/Photo Researchers, Inc. 188: (tr) E. R. Degginger/Photo Researchers, Inc. 189: Craig K. Lorenz/Photo Researchers, Inc. 190: (tl) Randy Wells/CORBIS; (tc) David M. Schleser/Natures Images Inc./Photo Researchers, Inc; (b) Kim Heacox/Stone/Getty Images, Inc; (bl) Diana L. Stratton/Tom Stack and Associates. 191: (t) M. H. Sharp/Photo Researchers, Inc; (cl) M. H. Sharp/ Photo Researchers, Inc; (br) Joe McDonald/Visuals Unlimited. 192:(c) Courtesy Scholastic; (l) SuperStock; (cr) Superstock; (r) Gary Meszaros/ Dembinsky Photo Associates. 192-193: Raymond Gehman/CORBIS. 193:(tc) M. H. Sharp/Photo Researchers, Inc; (b) Kim Heacox/Stone/ Getty Images, Inc. 194: Lawrence Manning/CORBIS. 195: Philippe McClelland/Stone/Getty Images, Inc. 196: (tr) Siede Preis/Getty Images, Inc; (b) Agnes Overbaugh. 197: Rick Friedman/CORBIS. 198: Diana L. Stratton/Tom Stack and Associates. 199: Superstock/Alamy. 200-201: Karl Ammann/NPL/Minden Pictures. 202: Gerry Ellis/Minden Pictures. 203: (t row) ZSSD/Minden Pictures; Tom & Pat Leeson/Photo Researchers; (center row l to r) Tim Fitzharris/Minden Pictures; Suzanne L and Joseph T. Collins/Photo Researchers; James Hanken/ Bruce Coleman; Tom and Pat Leeson/Photo Researchers; (br) Stephen Richards. 204: Yva Momatiuk/John Eastcott/Minden Pictures. 205: (t to b) Norbert Rosing/NGS Image Collection; Tui de Roy/Minden Pictures. 206: AP Photo/Anchorage Daily News/Jim Lavakas. 207: Jonathan Bird/ Peter Arnold. 208: (t to b) Mark Newman/Photo Researchers; Stefan Myers/Okapia/Photo Researchers. 211: (bl) Lars Lindblad/Shutterstock; (b) Tracy Montana/PhotoLink/Getty Images. 212-213: Chuck Place/Place Stock. 214: (tr) G.K. & Vikki Hart/Getty Images, Inc; (bl) Premium Stock/ CORBIS. 215: Juniors Bildarchiv/Alamy. 228:(tl) Photo by Donald E. Johnson; (bl) Courtesy Estate of Garth Williams c/o Frost National Bank. 233: Royalty-Free/CORBIS. 234-235: Konrad Wothe/Minden Pictures. 236-237: FogStock LLC. 237: Creatas/PunchStock. 238-239: Robert Franz/Jupiter Images. 240: Photos.com/Jupiter Images. 241: Stockbyte/PunchStock. 242: Photos.com/Jupiter Images. 243: Photos. com/Jupiter Images. 244: Heidi & Hans-Jurgen Koch/Minden Pictures. 245: Pete Oxford/Minden Pictures. 246: J. Mallwitz/Peter Arnold, Inc. 247: Tom Boyden/Lonely Planet Images. 248: Designpics.com/ PunchStock. 249: (t) AGE Fotostock/SuperStock; (b) Photos.com/ Jupiter Images. 250: David A. Northcott/CORBIS. 251: Yva Momatiuk & John Eastcott/Minden Pictures. 252-253: Jeff Vanuga/CORBIS/Jupiter Images. 253: Galen Rowell/CORBIS. 254: Photos.com/Jupiter Images. 255: Photos.com/Jupiter Images. 256: Michael & Patricia Fogden/ CORBIS. 257: Joe McDonald/CORBIS. 258: (b) Photos.com/Jupiter Images; (c) Photos.com. 259: Photos.com/Jupiter Images. 260: (cr) Courtesy of Kathy Pintair; (cl) Thomas Kitchin & Victoria Hurst. 260-261: Photos.com/Jupiter Images. 266: Corel Corporation. 267: Photodisc Blue/Getty Images, Inc. 270: (t) Gene Rhoden/Alamy; (br) Jim Reed Photography. 271: Gene Rhoden/Alamy. 274-275: Randy Faris/Corbis. 275: Grant Faint. 276: Burazin/Masterfile. 277: Miriam Berkeley. 278-279: George Shelley/AGE footstock. 280: Brand X Pictures/Getty Images, Inc. 280-281: The Image Bank/Getty Images, Inc. 281: (tr) N/ Felicia Martinez/Photo Edit Inc; (cr) Spike Mafford/Getty Images, Inc. 302: Courtesy Scholastic. 304: (l) Photodisc/Getty Images, Inc; (bc) Greg Kuchik/Getty Images, Inc. 304-305: foodfolio/Alamy. 306: (l) Photodisc/Getty Images, Inc; (tc) Jon Burbank/The Image Works, Inc; (bl) Foodpix. 306-307: Foodfolio/Alamy. 309: Bryan Peterson/Getty Images, Inc. 310-311: Digital Vision/Getty Images. 328: (tr) Michael Greenlar: Courtesy Joseph Bruchac; (br) Courtesy Lucia Angela Perez. 330-331: (t) Rick Fischer; (b) Bill Frymire. 332-333: Bill Frymire. 335: Holos/Getty Images, Inc. 336-337: (spread) Tim Graham/Getty Images. 338: Tom Raymond/Fresh Air Photographics. 339: (b) Mary Evans Picture Library/Everett Collection. 342: courtesy Robert Greygrass. 343: courtesy Rose Red Elk. 344: Library of Congress, Prints & Photographs Division, FSA/OWI Collection. 347: (c) Bet Noire/Shutterstock; (r) Stockbyte/PunchStock; (b) Ryan McVay/Getty Images. 348-349: Larry Dale Gordon/Getty Images. 376: Courtesy Susan Stevens Crummel. 378: Comstock Images/Alamy. 379: Premium Stock/CORBIS. 380: (tl) N/ Foodpix; (br) Royalty Free/CORBIS. 381: Steve Niedorf Photography/The Image Bank/Getty Images, Inc. 383: Pierre Arsenault/Masterfile. 384-385: Bill Aron/Photo Edit. 386: Robert Dowling/CORBIS. 404: (tr) Courtesy Lauren Thompson; (c) Courtesy Linda S. Wingerter. 411: Royalty-Free/CORBIS. 414: Lynda Richardson/CORBIS. 415: BRECK P. KENT/Animals Animals - Earth Scenes. 418: (br) Robert Glusic/Getty Images, Inc; (bl) Creatas/Picture Quest. 420: Stock Connection Blue/ Alamy. 421: (br) PhotoAlto/Picture Quest; (bl) Robert Glusic/Getty Images, Inc. 424: Creatas/Picture Quest. 425: David Young-Wolff / PhotoEdit. 426: DAJ. 427: (l) Siede Preis/Getty Images Inc; Digital Vision/PunchStock. 428: Photolink/Getty Images, Inc. 429: Mehau Kulyk/Photo Researchers, Inc. 431: FoodCollection Royalty Free Photograph/PunchStock - Upper Cut Images. IBC: MedioImages/Getty Images.

# Reading/Language Arts
# CA California Standards
## Grade 3

## READING

### 1.0 Word Analysis, Fluency, and Systematic Vocabulary Development
Students understand the basic features of reading. They select letter patterns and know how to translate them into spoken language by using phonics, syllabication, and word parts. They apply this knowledge to achieve fluent oral and silent reading.

### Decoding and Word Recognition

| | |
|---|---|
| 1.1 | Know and use complex word families when reading (e.g., *-ight*) to decode unfamiliar words. |
| 1.2 | Decode regular multisyllabic words. |
| 1.3 | Read aloud narrative and expository text fluently and accurately and with appropriate pacing, intonation, and expression. |

### Vocabulary and Concept Development

| | |
|---|---|
| 1.4 | Use knowledge of antonyms, synonyms, homophones, and homographs to determine the meanings of words. |
| 1.5 | Demonstrate knowledge of levels of specificity among grade-appropriate words and explain the importance of these relations (e.g., *dog/ mammal/ animal/ living things*). |
| 1.6 | Use sentence and word context to find the meaning of unknown words. |
| 1.7 | Use a dictionary to learn the meaning and other features of unknown words. |
| 1.8 | Use knowledge of prefixes (e.g., *un-, re-, pre-, bi-, mis-, dis-*) and suffixes (e.g., *-er, -est, -ful*) to determine the meaning of words. |

### 2.0 Reading Comprehension
Students read and understand grade-level-appropriate material. They draw upon a variety of comprehension strategies as needed (e.g., generating and responding to essential questions, making predictions, comparing information from several sources). The selections in *Recommended Literature, Kindergarten Through Grade Twelve* illustrate the quality and complexity of the materials to be read by students. In addition to their regular school reading, by grade four, students read one-half million words annually, including a good representation of grade-level-appropriate narrative and expository text (e.g., classic and contemporary literature, magazines, newspapers, online information). In grade three, students make substantial progress toward this goal.

## READING (continued)

### Structural Features of Informational Materials

| 2.1 | Use titles, tables of contents, chapter headings, glossaries, and indexes to locate information in text. |
|---|---|

### Comprehension and Analysis of Grade-Level-Appropriate Text

| 2.2 | Ask questions and support answers by connecting prior knowledge with literal information found in, and inferred from, the text. |
|---|---|
| 2.3 | Demonstrate comprehension by identifying answers in the text. |
| 2.4 | Recall major points in the text and make and modify predictions about forthcoming information. |
| 2.5 | Distinguish the main idea and supporting details in expository text. |
| 2.6 | Extract appropriate and significant information from the text, including problems and solutions. |
| 2.7 | Follow simple multiple-step written instructions (e.g., how to assemble a product or play a board game). |

**3.0 Literary Response and Analysis** Students read and respond to a wide variety of significant works of children's literature. They distinguish between the structural features of the text and literary terms or elements (e.g., theme, plot, setting, characters). The selections in *Recommended Literature, Kindergarten Through Grade Twelve* illustrate the quality and complexity of the materials to be read by students.

### Structural Features of Literature

| 3.1 | Distinguish common forms of literature (e.g., poetry, drama, fiction, nonfiction). |
|---|---|

### Narrative Analysis of Grade-Level-Appropriate Text

| 3.2 | Comprehend basic plots of classic fairy tales, myths, folktales, legends, and fables from around the world. |
|---|---|
| 3.3 | Determine what characters are like by what they say or do and by how the author or illustrator portrays them. |
| 3.4 | Determine the underlying theme or author's message in fiction and nonfiction text. |
| 3.5 | Recognize the similarities of sounds in words and rhythmic patterns (e.g., alliteration, onomatopoeia) in a selection. |
| 3.6 | Identify the speaker or narrator in a selection. |

## WRITING

**1.0 Writing Strategies** Students write clear and coherent sentences and paragraphs that develop a central idea. Their writing shows they consider the audience and purpose. Students progress through the stages of the writing process (e.g., prewriting, drafting, revising, editing successive versions).

### Organization and Focus

1.1 Create a single paragraph:
 a. Develop a topic sentence.
 b. Include simple supporting facts and details.

### Penmanship

1.2 Write legibly in cursive or joined italic, allowing margins and correct spacing between letters in a word and words in a sentence.

### Research

1.3 Understand the structure and organization of various reference materials (e.g., dictionary, thesaurus, atlas, encyclopedia).

### Evaluation and Revision

1.4 Revise drafts to improve the coherence and logical progression of ideas by using an established rubric.

**2.0 Writing Applications (Genres and Their Characteristics)** Students write compositions that describe and explain familiar objects, events, and experiences. Student writing demonstrates a command of standard American English and the drafting, research, and organizational strategies outlined in Writing Standard 1.0.

*Using the writing strategies of grade three outlined in Writing Standard 1.0, students:*

2.1 Write narratives:
 a. Provide a context within which an action takes place.
 b. Include well-chosen details to develop the plot.
 c. Provide insight into why the selected incident is memorable.

2.2 Write descriptions that use concrete sensory details to present and support unified impressions of people, places, things, or experiences.

2.3 Write personal and formal letters, thank-you notes, and invitations:
 a. Show awareness of the knowledge and interests of the audience and establish a purpose and context.
 b. Include the date, proper salutation, body, closing, and signature.

## WRITTEN AND ORAL ENGLISH LANGUAGE CONVENTIONS

The standards for written and oral English language conventions have been placed between those for writing and for listening and speaking because these conventions are essential to both sets of skills.

**1.0 Written and Oral English Language Conventions** Students write and speak with a command of standard English conventions appropriate to this grade level.

### Sentence Structure

1.1 Understand and be able to use complete and correct declarative, interrogative, imperative, and exclamatory sentences in writing and speaking.

### Grammar

1.2 Identify subjects and verbs that are in agreement and identify and use pronouns, adjectives, compound words, and articles correctly in writing and speaking.

1.3 Identify and use past, present, and future verb tenses properly in writing and speaking.

1.4 Identify and use subjects and verbs correctly in speaking and writing simple sentences.

### Punctuation

1.5 Punctuate dates, city and state, and titles of books correctly.

1.6 Use commas in dates, locations, and addresses and for items in a series.

### Capitalization

1.7 Capitalize geographical names, holidays, historical periods, and special events correctly.

### Spelling

1.8 Spell correctly one-syllable words that have blends, contractions, compounds, orthographic patterns (e.g., *qu*, consonant doubling, changing the ending of a word from -y to -ies when forming the plural), and common homophones (e.g., *hair-hare*).

1.9 Arrange words in alphabetic order.

## LISTENING AND SPEAKING

**1.0 Listening and Speaking Strategies** Students listen critically and respond appropriately to oral communication. They speak in a manner that guides the listener to understand important ideas by using proper phrasing, pitch, and modulation.

### Comprehension

1.1 Retell, paraphrase, and explain what has been said by a speaker.

1.2 Connect and relate prior experiences, insights, and ideas to those of a speaker.

1.3 Respond to questions with appropriate elaboration.

1.4 Identify the musical elements of literary language (e.g., rhymes, repeated sounds, instances of onomatopoeia).

### Organization and Delivery of Oral Communication

1.5 Organize ideas chronologically or around major points of information.

1.6 Provide a beginning, a middle, and an end, including concrete details that develop a central idea.

1.7 Use clear and specific vocabulary to communicate ideas and establish the tone.

1.8 Clarify and enhance oral presentations through the use of appropriate props (e.g., objects, pictures, charts).

1.9 Read prose and poetry aloud with fluency, rhythm, and pace, using appropriate intonation and vocal patterns to emphasize important passages of the text being read.

### Analysis and Evaluation of Oral and Media Communications

1.10 Compare ideas and points of view expressed in broadcast and print media.

1.11 Distinguish between the speaker's opinions and verifiable facts.

**2.0 Speaking Applications (Genres and Their Characteristics)** Students deliver brief recitations and oral presentations about familiar experiences or interests that are organized around a coherent thesis statement. Student speaking demonstrates a command of standard American English and the organizational and delivery strategies outlined in Listening and Speaking Standard 1.0.

*Using the speaking strategies of grade three outlined in Listening and Speaking Standard 1.0, students:*

2.1 Make brief narrative presentations:
   a. Provide a context for an incident that is the subject of the presentation.
   b. Provide insight into why the selected incident is memorable.
   c. Include well-chosen details to develop character, setting, and plot.

2.2 Plan and present dramatic interpretations of experiences, stories, poems, or plays with clear diction, pitch, tempo, and tone.

2.3 Make descriptive presentations that use concrete sensory details to set forth and support unified impressions of people, places, things, or experiences.